PLAIN STORIES
by a
GRANDPA

PLAIN STORIES by a GRANDPA

Translated by Renee H. Park

First published in 2024
by Hollym International Corp., Carlsbad, CA, USA
Phone 760 814 9880
www.hollym.com **e-Mail** contact@hollym.com

Published simultaneously in Korea
by Hollym Corp., Publishers, Seoul, Korea
Phone +82 2 734 5087 **Fax** +82 2 730 5149
www.hollym.net **e-Mail** hollym@hollym.co.kr

ISBN: 978-1-56591-525-1
Library of Congress Control Number: 2024936175

Printed in Korea

JUNG-KI "ROCKY" PARK

PLAIN STORIES by a GRANDPA

Translated by Renee H. Park

Hollym
Carlsbad, CA and Seoul

This book is dedicated to and written for my four beloved granddaughters: Hae-June Han, Renee Hyo Jung Park, Hyo Sung Park, and Hae-Yeon Han.

Table of Contents

Chapter 4

On Training Your Body

Chapter 5

Giving Back to Society

Foreword

My wife gave birth to my two children during the early days of our marriage. The town we lived in was Seoseok-dong, Gwangju. From our home, we could see Chosun University in the far-off distance.

My eldest was Tae-Jin. Fifteen months later, Hyun-Sun came into the world. I had my children by the age of twenty-nine, and even back then, this was considered relatively young.

One day, when I returned from work and went into the bedroom, I saw the two of them sleeping. I felt strongly then, "Of course, I am the father of both these young souls…how great is my responsibility!" Along with this infinite sense of responsibility, I first felt the self-awareness of being a father.

Years passed. After several moves, we relocated to Seoul, in the northern part of Ahyeon-dong. One day, I opened the door to the main bedroom and was momentarily taken aback. Two little girls, one from my son and the other from my daughter, lay sleeping.

All of a sudden, I felt a rush of emotions, but one that differed from the ones I had felt as a new father long ago. Instead of feelings, what I felt, felt more like shock. I gazed at my two granddaughters for a long time.

How could I describe these feelings—rather than responsibility, I felt deeply moved—that I had done my duty and thus felt a certain sense of satisfaction coupled with an innate sense of gratitude. I said to myself, "Thanks be to God," almost automatically.

"Dear grandchildren, where have you come from?"

I asked this question, as one living being, asking two others. Of course, it was soul-to-soul.

I imagined them replying, "From Heaven!"

"My little ones, I am not your father, but your grandfather. There are too many things I must do for both of you."

This wave of duty crashed over me, but at the same time, it was tempered by love.

"So this is a grandfather's love," I thought.

That is why, from then on, I kept on thinking of things I should do for both of them. They had not asked for this, nor had anyone insisted on it, but I felt pressed to act.

The answer struck me. "That's right! I should write a book. In order to live and thrive in this harsh world, they must have wisdom. To these two grandchildren, I should advise them on how to live, and live correctly."

I had not even thought of writing a book before. That I, a mere man, would write a book! Surprisingly enough, however, this task fell to me, rather than to another person. It became my new mission.

It was difficult. There were highs and lows. There were some days when I wanted to give up.

After ten months of writing, and none of them easy, this book came to see the light of day.

March 2018

Chapter 1

What Defines Humanity

●●

Give Glory to Life

"A predator chases an itinerant wanderer on an open field. Right before the savage beast catches the wanderer, he finds a well. Hastily, he grabs at vines and enters it. A little while later, while starting to descend down the well, he can feel the breath of the beast near his head. He almost panics and looks up. He can see into the red mouth of the beast. He has to catch his breath while panic wells up in him. The beast is growling, but cannot enter the place where he is. That is when the itinerant wanderer closes his eyes and sighs with relief.

He decides to descend further down the well, to escape the beast, and uses the vine he's holding onto to rappel down the well. As the surface of the well nears, he can see something twisting and writhing. He looks closer. But what is this! A large serpent is gazing up at him, coiled and ready to strike at a moment's notice.

The itinerant wanderer is chilled to the bone. He stops in his tracks.

When he gazes up, the beast is still nearby, with his mouth open wide. At the floor of the dry well, there is a large serpent, writhing and twisting, staring at him with large eyes. The itinerant wanderer is stuck between a rock and a hard place.

Though he's struck dumb, he tries to quiet his fears and closes his eyes and breathes deeply. Then he holds the vine tightly. If he loses his grip, then all is lost. Time passes in fear and desperation.

There is a rustling sound somewhere. When he opens his eyes, he sees a small mouse that is gnawing on the vine he is holding. The itinerant wanderer feels like the sky is crashing around his shoulders. So this is it, he thinks. He closes his eyes and presses his lips together. So the end is coming, just like this. He feels a sinking sense of despair.

At this moment, something touches his lips. Carefully, he licks them. It's sweet. On the vine's leaves, there is honey. The itinerant wanderer temporarily forgets about the beast, the poisonous snake, and the mouse, and licks the honey from the leaves. Such is life."

This is a retelling of a Buddhist narrative from Tolstoy's *On Life*. So are our lives to be spent, rappelling down the well chased by a beast and waiting to be poisoned by a serpent? In Europe, this may be the case, as with depressing Slavic folklore. Before us, there is a savage beast and a poisonous serpent. On the plain, there is a brook and a hill that is warmed by the sun. Deer jumps about in joy on the green plains, while the sun shines too.

According to Greek mythology, when Zeus first made a female, he named her Pandora. Pandora means, "she who has received all (gifts)." This first female's creation had the hand of many gods. Some gave her beauty, others, the gift of music…

Pandora marries Epimetheus, the younger brother of Prometheus, who gifted mankind with fire.

Epimetheus had a box that he had treasured for a long while, and in the box, were all sorts of societal ills. It was full of them.

The ever-curious Pandora, one day, despite all of our protestations, opened the box. Then all the ills plaguing mankind today including resentment, revenge, and jealousy all spewed forth and spread to the four corners of the Earth.

Pandora, who was quite alarmed by this point, closed the box hurriedly but everything had already left, with the exception of "hope."

That is why to this day, man has to live with all sorts of terrible, painful things, but the last and the best of these all is the all-abiding sense of hope.

This is true. The worst thing in life is to despair. Never, ever lose hope.

This may be a similar metaphor to "a frog in a well" metaphor, but to the itinerant wanderer, did he not have God and did he not have faith?

The world may be full of pain, but hope abides. What we are called to do is to hope, and praise the Lord for all His glory.

What Is Life?

Hae-June and Hyo Jung, a person knows many things. This is also why we question, because the more we know the less we know.

One of the most common questions that have been asked over and over again is, "What is life?" At least, this is my understanding. Thousands of years have passed since we first started asking this, and yet we have not arrived at an answer.

Hyo Sung, Hae-Yeon, I hope you don't spend a lot of time pondering this conundrum in the years to come. But there is one question I would like for you two to ponder. It is not, "What is life," but rather, "How should a person lead his life?"

Instead of distinguishing between the sound of a hammer or the stone, you must ponder how to use the hammer, and what to use it for.

In my opinion, the purpose of life is "to work on one's own faults while putting others at an advantage." The first part of this message is to study, which will elevate the intellect, then work with a firm resolve. These three parts, when practiced and used, must work in harmony.

Even though our society already has advanced the humanities, the world is still topsy-turvy, and tragedies abound because we have not worked on these three qualities, in my humble opinion.

Once upon a time, long ago, when people were more ignorant than they are now, we gazed with wonder at the twinkling night stars in the Heavens. When we first believed in deities, we must have sought comfort and peace.

But the reasons for scientific study must have arisen at some point in time, and rationale and logic and reason have been at the forefront of our minds for some time now. Is this because we sought the knowledge behind the pitch-black night and because we were frightened by thunder and lightning?

The world of logic was born by Copernicus[•] and Descartes[••] worked to disprove his predecessor's idea of the Sun revolving around Earth rather than the other way around. People started to believe in modern science. The reason behind this was because science really gifted us with many things. The wisdom to be gleaned from this is that science really rules the universe. That is why science, at times, may seem more powerful than our belief in God.

With the advent of the Age of Enlightenment, we started to place

• Poland's astronomer and Catholic saint Nicolaus Copernicus (1473–1543) said that the planets revolved around the sun, and caused shockwaves throughout the scholastic community during that time.

•• Rene Descartes (1596–1650) was a French philosopher, mathematician, and a driving force behind modern science and philosophy. One of his most important contributions includes "the scientific method."

more emphasis on the mind and advanced studies. This led to the abandonment, at times, of more ephemeral qualities like the soul. We even began to question our beliefs in God and in angels. Our downfall, perhaps, started with this. We should have heeded the warnings of the French philosopher and mathematician we call Pascal.•

So what is behind self-discipline? The *Talmud*•• may have some answers for us.

"People who surpass others may not truly be exceptional. The one who surpasses his former self is the exceptional one."

This concept is also found in our wise ancient Asian text, the *Book of Changes*, which also talks about the art of self-discipline. "Ceaseless endeavors" towards self-discipline is the most important.

How can we apply this to the real world?

The first is to cultivate the right "heart." This includes humility and filial piety, along with the love for God.

The second is through study. A person must learn in order to realize things. Without learning and understanding, a person will be unable to do his duty.

The third is having the right mindset. A person must be able to distinguish between right and wrong. This "moral compass" is found in an ancient text called, "The good things for the world." What is good for thy neighbor and what is good for the society at large is the pretext of this at play.

For God, we can make a better world, and He sent us to the Earth in

• Blaise Pascal (1623–1662) was a French philosopher and mathematician that was responsible for the masterpiece, *Pensées*, where he explores the contradictions of human nature.

•• The *Talmud* is a collection of Jewish texts that explores law, philosophy, and how to interpret parts of the Jewish Bible.

order to help others.

What is good for the society at large? At times, it may include good deeds and volunteering and working for the government.

This does not mean that one has to run away to Africa like Schweitzer,• however. A kind word for a friend to helping those in financial distress...all these small acts of kindness are examples of benefiting others.

Ghandi once got on a train that was ready to depart. At that moment, he lost a shoe on the train platform. The train was already moving, and Ghandi couldn't pick up his shoe. At that moment, Ghandi threw his remaining shoe onto the platform. A shoe is useless without its pair, and someone could make use of them if he had two rather than one shoe.

"Life is the belief that for someone else, I become a coal briquette."

One Korean poet named Ahn Do-Hyun once sang this. Remember, these acts of kindness are not measured by grandiosity.

To treat one's neighbor as oneself, to refrain from doing things that may harm others are all examples of this.

It is difficult, I admit, to put others first.

Hae-June, Hyo Jung, this is a law unto society that has been followed since Christ's arrival on Earth. Admiral Yi Sun-sin of Korea is another such example, and the twinkling stars in the sky attest to everyone's sacrifices, at one point or another.

• Albert Schweitzer (1875–1965) was a German doctor, philosopher, and humanitarian who left his home to become a missionary in Africa from 1913 onwards. He spent the majority of his life advancing medicine and Christianity there. In 1952, he won the Nobel Peace Prize.

We owe a lot to others, from time immortal. Sometimes these debts to others cannot be repaid.

What is really important is to keep this in mind, from the very beginning.

"A family that gives alms to the poor will have prosperous descendants." That is why it is good to do good, and it all starts with the adults of the family.

When we examine noble families, we can note that their ancestors did many good things. This can be found in the West as well as the East.

Of course, working for the good of others means that one will not see the success of one's labors right away. It will be difficult, time consuming, and tiring, and sometimes, you will have to use your own money. But do not shy away from this task. If there is a way for you to help, do not hesitate. Help to the best of your ability. This is the cornerstone of a healthy society.

How one lives his life becomes the difference between a mouse in the gutter and an eagle, soaring high above.

Filial Piety

Hyo Sung and Hae-Yeon, if everyone is to live in this world, and keep it good, then there are some standards that everyone must follow.

This difficult world can be traversed through a type of moral philosophy. Basically, it boils down to "how to [best] live one's life." This is something you will carry with you everywhere.

To keep your standards high you must reflect upon your own

misdeeds and repent. There is a moral code, or a "yardstick" to live by. Our forefathers, the sage ones, at least, espoused the "*sāngāngwǔlún* (Three Fundamental Principles and Five Moral Disciplines)." This comes from the Chinese. The first part of this phrase refers to relationships; for example, between the King and subject, the relationship between father and son, and the relationship between husband and wife.

The second part of this Chinese phrase refers to the people: the king, son, spouses, elders, and friends. The relationships between them are governed by certain societal and moral codes.

I am only going to talk about a few of these, because these teachings are from the ancient past, and in this modern age and time, there are some that will not fit today's standards.

For example, in this era of motor vehicles, you'd be hard pressed to travel via carriage, unless you have a specific reason.

These old teachings are not really without structure, and as such, they can be tailored to one's individual mindset. Even for today's time and that to follow; time perennial. At least, this is my thinking.

Let me introduce the concept of filial piety, while we're on this topic.

When our ancestors were young, everyone had to learn the book called *Sohak*.• This book dates back to the Song Dynasty of China and edited for children's use. Eight hundred years have passed since this time, but a person's duty and behavior can still be modeled after these teachings.

These days, young people, when they read the *Sohak*, think it's outdated and refuse to accept its teachings.

• *Sohak* was written by Chu Hsi, of the Song Dynasty, and contains codes of conduct regarding manners and good deeds. It is considered one of the best books from the Song Dynasty to date.

Hyo Jung and Hyo Sung, your father also complained about the *Sohak* when he first read it. He said at least half of it didn't make sense. This was back in high school, so no wonder why, I thought at the time (and still do). But when and if he reads the book again, I am sure he will think differently.

One's duty, or "dori," and life's truths cannot be solved like a mathematical problem, and is difficult to understand. This is because it is not knowledge, but wisdom. When you are my age, I hope you understand the deeper meaning behind the *Sohak*.

The *Sohak* is centuries old, as I have stated before, but its teachings have been put into practice in the East at least for two thousand years, and taught by the sages as well.

When reading it, let us be reminded of how brilliant our ancestors were, all those years ago.

You may have become impatient with Grandpa by now, for I keep on droning on about classical Chinese texts. But remember, along with India and Greece, China is another place where human civilization started.

Rejecting something because it is foreign to you is a silly idea. Are you going to abandon Christianity because Jesus Christ was Jewish?

Good deeds and good works demand praise not censure, no matter their place of origin.

Grandpa would like to discuss with you several teachings regarding filial piety in the *Sohak*. I am afraid of telling you what to do when I have such brilliant predecessors who outlined it in books already.

A son, when taking care of his parents, should make sure that the room and their clothing are warm during the winters. During the summers, they must be cool, and at night, the futon should be laid out and put to use. At dawn, he should inquire as to whether they have slept well. When leaving the house, he should inform them, and upon returning, he should also inform them and note the color of his parents' cheeks. Play should only happen in so far as it doesn't worry his parents, and he should study hard and grow into a fine young man, so that he may delight his parents. In front of his parents, he must almost never mention that he is old.

A man who loves his parents is always surrounded by a good aura. A good aura denotes a pleasant demeanor and a happy glow, and this will contribute to a good attitude. A man who honors his parents will, like holding a precious white jade in his palm, or holding a bowl full of water, will always take caution. Take note of people who are too strict and dangerous and serious, for they are not honoring and taking care of their parents.

In olden times, when a king did wrong, the subject was exhorted, and when the parents did wrong, the son remonstrated. In the case of a king, when he did wrong three times, then the subject would leave, but in the case of parents, even after three times, the son cried and had to follow their will.

Those who honor their parents will never be full of arrogance, no matter how high their station in life, and even at a lower station, will not cause a disturbance. In the case of the latter, he will not fight with his brethren but instead, get along with them.

If the actions that a person takes at home are not good, then it goes against the concept of filial piety, and if one does not pledge his loyalty to his king, then it also goes against filial piety. A government official who does wrong harms his parents as well. If trust is broken between friends, then they also dishonor their parents.

Lao• has two fathers, both of whom he holds in high esteem. He is seventy years old, but like a child, he is playful and wears a garment made with the colors of the rainbow.

During the Han Dynasty of China, there once lived a man named Hanboyu. He was renowned throughout the land for his filial piety.

One day, he had made some transgression or another, and his mother took up a stick and started beating him.

Boyu cried. His mother said, "On other days, you did not cry, even when I hit you with this stick. But what ails you today?"

Boyu replied, "Before, your beatings always hurt. But today, it doesn't hurt. I cry because you're weakened and have lost your former strength."

Children, are you getting frustrated yet? I am not going to add another word to this tale. But even after centuries, these lessons hold true, even today, even for you youngsters.

So why am I discussing love for one's parents as central to a person's nature?

There are academics, the country, and God, to think of, and yet, why do I put parents first?

A person must truly love another. When a person loves, he becomes calmer and more truthful, and more prudent and more likely to sacrifice for others.

In this world, there is no greater person than Mother. This is due to

• Lao was a contemporary of Confucius, from the Spring and Autumn Period in Chinese history. He avoided the turbulence of war and anarchy, and chose to be a farmer instead. When the king summoned him to court after hearing of his wisdom, he did not go. People congregated around him, wherever he went. He is the author of fifteen books.

her maternal love. Where else in this world can you find a greater love than the love that a mother has for her children? That is why a mother is calm and truthful and always sacrificing for her children.

Along the same lines, once a person is born and learns to love his parents, then, "He will move with solemnity, pledge loyalty to his country, and stay true to his friends."

This type of love sets us apart and is integral to what it means to be human. Is it not the virtue of virtues, to love one's parents?

I always remember Corinthians every time I read the *Sohak*.

In 1 Corinthians 13:4–6, it says, "Love is patient, love is kind. It does not envy. It does not boast, it is not proud. It is not rude, it is not self-seeking, it is not easily angered, it keeps no record of wrongs."

In the *Sohak*, it says, "A person who practices filial piety is not proud, does not fight, keeps the peace, acts with propriety, and is loyal to his country."

Are these phrases not similar?

Jesus Christ, through love, and the *Sohak*, through filial piety, teach us the right path towards God. West or East, the truth remains the truth.

Hyo Jung, love your mother and father more than you love your king. Hae-June, love your parents as though your heart is breaking, for their corporeal punishments are no longer as strong as before.

Husband and Wife

When discussing Chinese history, there are two figures, "Yao" and "Shun," who are almost always mentioned whenever the subject turns to virtuous Kings.•

This king, surnamed Yao, bequeathed more to "Shun" than to his own son. King Yao bade Shun to marry his daughter, observed how well he handled her, then granted him the keys to the kingdom (the throne).

A married couple starts a family, and this is a microcosm of how a king handles his subjects in a country. Creating a happy, contented family is paramount to ruling over a kingdom, do you not agree?

That is why Lin Yutang•• writes that with all things being equal, "the family unit is the most precious out of all organizations, truthful from a scientific perspective, and is biologically sound." No other human groups or organizations can compare.

We do not have to turn to the classics or important people in order to realize this. A family is what we are born to, and where we eat, grow up, and learn. All fights dissipate in the presence of a maternal love everlasting, where peace and God also reign supreme.

It is my personal belief that there is no afterlife, i.e., Heaven. I choose to believe, instead, that the family is where you can find Heaven on Earth. I bear no ill will even if there is no fantastic afterlife.

But to be sure, not all families are like Heaven. In order to make the family unit a Heaven of sorts, then two stalwart figures supporting it must be the husband and the wife.

How can they create Heaven?

Many of our ancestors have had much to say about this subject, but I think one theme prevails over a lot of others. What am I referring to?

• "Yao" and "Shun" are thought to be the amalgamation of several kings and are more legend than a true historical figure.

•• Lin Yutang (1895–1976) was a Chinese literary critic and writer.

It is love. A truthful love. We may talk of love, but the concept itself is difficult. Why? Real love is different from what many warble about.

Love that only gives without expecting anything in return, that's real love. But unconditional love, is that possible?

No, most will not understand this concept, so they cannot put it into practice.

Thoughts differ, feelings differ, and chimerical emotions define man. A love between a man and a woman is what most people commonly refer to as love. Similar to a roaring flame of fire, yet as delicate as glass. It will expire at some point and will break at another point in time.

There are married couples who do not understand the concept of unconditional love. That is why these days, there are statistics that say, for example, that one in three couples will eventually divorce.

Then what should we do?

I myself do not have the answer. Isn't this problematic? It's a problem for Grandpa too. But do not worry. If I don't have the answer, you can always turn to the sages.

"Love never gives up, never loses faith, is always hopeful, and endures through every circumstance."•

This is an example of genuine love. How beautiful and honorable. This is the word of the Lord.

Without this type of unconditional, genuine love, a couple cannot make a family like Heaven. This isn't easy. With most people, they are not up to the task for they put in too little effort.

Then how can you keep silent, believe, and keep on hoping?

Hae-June and Hyo Jung, both of you may dislike what I'm about to

• Jacob, because he loved Rachel, lived as an indentured servant for fourteen years. This is found in 1 Corinthians 13:7.

say, but first of all, a wife has to respect her husband.

Grandpa always told your aunt, Hyo Jung, that once she marries, then she must revere her husband as a god. This is not because he is exceptional. This is not because he is a man. It is because he is her husband. This will keep the family together. This will make a Heaven out of family life.

It does not matter if your husband is unexceptional. Think of Princess Pyeonggang and Foolish Ondal. The lesson to be learned here is that if the husband and wife love each other, then Ondal becomes a renowned general.

I don't want to give a long explanation about this. Even if this is difficult, follow Grandpa's advice. This will lead to Heaven (on Earth), and with the passage of time, you will understand what I meant by this.

I am now warning the men of this family in the years to come. If you want to be respected by your wife and receive her unconditional support, remember that she holds the keys to the very foundation of the marriage itself.

In one of the ancient Chinese classics, there is a saying that I hold dear to my heart. It goes like this: "If the family finances are suffering, then think of a miserly wife, and if the nation goes topsy-turvy, then think of your benevolent Prime Minister."•

"A woman's keen intuition surpasses a proud man's supposed knowledge," so says Ghandi.

The very foundation of the family is the wife; this is what the men of this family must hold dear in their hearts.

• During the Han Dynasty of China, one of the kings said this in a history book.

Brotherly Love

My mother died in 1984 when she was eighty-six years old. While she was still alive, she would often quote wise adages and provide examples of this.

I will now recount a story about brotherly love that you can think back upon often.

Once upon a time, a long time ago, lived two brothers. One day, the younger brother killed a pig, and while the blood was still dripping from his head, he wrapped the victim in cloth and went to his most trustworthy friend.

"Friend, I accidentally killed a man. Can you help me?"

As soon as he said this, the friend's face turned ashen and slammed the door on him. The younger brother turned around and went to another close friend. He said the same thing. This second friend turned his back on him and shoved him out the door.

At the end of the road, the younger brother went to his older brother and told him the truth. The astonished older brother grabbed his younger brother's arm and said to him, "How did you come to this? Hide yourself, the body, quickly, in my home. Then we will think this through, together."

This fable doesn't teach us not to respect and believe our friends. Human relations dictate that what we can expect from friends differ from that of our brothers. This is the lesson that we must learn.

I will repeat this again. No matter how strong the friendship is, there will be an invisible line that you cannot and should not cross, and this is the paramount lesson that you must learn. Between blood brothers, no matter how difficult, they must always forgive and accept all. It's a special relationship, is it not?

In the *Sohak*, which we have discussed before, a relationship between siblings consists of giving and receiving, and connectivity. When they are young, the parents hold their hands and bring them along to activities. While they are eating, they share a table, and share hand-me-downs when needed. When they learn, they study together and when they wish to play, they have a favorite place to go to. Suffice it to say that in my opinion, most siblings, even if they do not respect each other or do their utmost duty, love, or should love, each other.

This is what it means to be brothers. In this world, there are billions of people. But only a few share the same bloodline. This relationship between brothers, sisters, brothers and sisters, is unique and special unto itself.

If there is something to be shared, it must be shared amongst siblings, and if there are pleasant events, then they share their joy. If there are sad or difficult events, then they can share the burden to lessen the pain, and if there are difficult things that need to be addressed, they can use their combined power to their full advantage. In the case of difficulties and sad events, let it be known that it may be that only siblings understand the gravity of whatever it is that is ailing them.

As each person goes through life, he will encounter difficulties as well as happy events and sad events. When you are in a pickle, or so they say in the United States, it may be that you can extend your hand and ask for help from those surrounding you. This may come as a surprise, but trust me.

A man's human nature dictates that he will put himself first, then the family, then finally, others. That is why there's an adage saying, "My headache is more important than my neighbor's death, which occurred yesterday."

There are those who delight in others' pain. This is not surprising to me at all. This is sometimes unfortunately found in relationships between people.

This is why I stress kindness towards others. This will lead, hopefully, to the creation of a happier world, and a warmer society.

If you take the sibling relationship for granted, it may spoil, so they must take care of the relationship like pruning a tree.

If you need to grow a tree, then you must water it, give it fertilizer, and continue to take care of it.

How can you raise a tree? Through small, good deeds. This is a metaphor, of course. A kind word, a phone call, and a present of a necktie; these are small acts of kindness.

"Why are these small acts of kindness important? What use are they?" you may ask. But when you apply theory to practice, then you realize that these small acts of kindness are more difficult. Larger acts of kindness are easier. These larger acts of kindness require our patience and sacrifice just once, but for the other types, you are not able to do these without what Koreans call "jeongseong (sincere heart)."

That is why a single kind phrase, a small present of a necktie is not the point. The point is "jeongseong."

Additionally, the difficulty with the small acts of kindness is that it requires a certain finesse and tact.

The tree of relationships cannot grow without proper loving care, and without a feeling of doing good unto others, then there will be no brotherly love.

Children, Grandpa feels embarrassed for I have not always acted in this manner.

When I look back upon this, my mother used to say these kinds of adages to me, and yet, I did not.

Only at this have I come upon this realization, so I feel embarrassed about preaching to the choir, or to you angelic children.

In the *Sohak*, it mentions:

"When the brothers are of age, they marry and become the head of a household with a wife and children. This becomes the divisive and decisive line between 'mine' and 'yours' between brothers."

This is a remarkable observation, is it not? After all, good companionship between brothers and siblings takes a different turn once the sister gets married and once the brother takes a wife. This is a rule of society and one that you should heed carefully.

The biggest problem arises when there is too great a gap economically or with regard to social class between brothers.

If there is a difference between how learned they are, or if one suffers from an illness, then after middle age, there will be a rift between the brothers.

If one lacks education, then they will be unable to enter society and rise to dizzying heights; they will fall behind naturally. That means that the society that they end up joining will dictate their social class, and the easy conversation between the brothers will come to an end, for they will not understand each other's predicament.

That is why parents should work to provide an equal education for both brothers during the course of their childhood and adolescence, and beyond.

If they are both properly educated, then without taking into consideration their majors, and if they invest at least twenty years along the same line of work, then they will at least be upper-middle class.

This is the current societal strata dictated by society today.

If the elder brother eschews honor and focuses on making lots of money instead, then he will be commercially successful, and if the older sister has a high level of education, then the younger sister will marry a man from a good family. As such, everyone plays a role in how each will fare.

This all stems from education, so education I believe becomes the great equalizer. Let us remember this.

But what to do when there is too great a socio-economic rift between brothers?

Then one must have "jeongseong" and help the other in need. Think upon your father and your mother, and remember those times when you played together and also remember the times when you wept together and shared your grief. You must understand the other, help when you can, without any reservations, and the more financially/socially successful one should always help the one less fortunate.

To share does not always mean feelings or monetary assistance. You must spend time together as well. How can you effectively spend time together, and wisely, at that? It means to simply spend time together. You can take walks together, and if both are able to afford a vacation, then take a vacation together, and another easy way is to dine together. These methods will strengthen bonds between brothers, even after marriage. This is the best way.

A person's nature is an important matter of life. That is why people are born with certain traits. A person's duty is to his father, spouse, siblings, and friends, and you can see a person's nature come into action by observing how he behaves with all of them.

A person's true nature will dictate how he will behave in society.

However, sometimes you must go against your true nature or stretch it to its full limits, regardless of how you feel about it and even if it goes against your real temperament of wanting to win all the time.

I call upon everyone to leave pride behind and do away with the need to stand apart from the pack as the sole elite.

Chapter 2

Honesty Becomes You

Only the Strongest Survive

The Beautiful Virtues vs. Sinful Deeds

Be Religious

Only the Strongest Survive

In this world, only the strongest survive. Nature dictates this as a law. The strongest are the virtues while the weakest are the sins.

Whether you are physically strong or have wings, or have dithering feet, surviving means that you are adhering to one of the laws of nature.

As such, in order to survive as humans, we have to be strong. But what is the point in only surviving? We have to be better than the rest. Only then can we help others.

So, what are the prerequisites to being one of the strongest?

Your will, mindset, or heart. Prowess via physical strength, or having a high level of education is all good and well, but your mindset has to be strong. This denotes the strongest of the strong.

So what am I referring to, exactly?

Loving God, respecting human nature, having manners, appreciating Beauty, being brave, and being self-sacrificing at times; these are all part of having a strong mindset.

But what is at the core of making your mindset, willpower, or heart, clean?

It is honesty. A pure heart and a pure mindset. Then, you will not fool yourself or others.

Without honesty, all is lost, and all is pretense.

Where there is no honesty, there is no charm. If you are honest then you are always honorable. You will have a high level of self-esteem. In front of anyone and everyone, you will be full of self-confidence.

Unfortunately, in today's world, a little bit of talent and some liars seem to surpass those who are honest, the latter who are labeled as stupid. But even if sometimes you lose, I want to instill in you confidence behind what I am saying. As you grow older, you will realize that Grandpa was right all along.

Those who did well in their studies during college, or those who are so talented that they even appeared on foreigners' TV screens…these learned and talented people sometimes lag behind the honest ones.

This is all because of dishonesty.

As you grow older, you will realize that mere degrees and talents will never surpass those who are honest. If you are honest, you are confident, and this will place you first.

It is true that people tend to congregate around those who are with money or power. But beautiful flowers bloom then die ten days later, and a winning streak will never last for over ten years.

People also congregate around honest people. Why? Because humans are naturally drawn to honesty, and they will support it as well. Lies will fall apart quickly, while what is naturally good will not tarnish.

A good person will shine with virtue. This is the "light from within." Or, "the scent of the heart," as they say in Korea.

What do I mean by this? A good person will be resplendent with a regal bearing.

This light will warm your heart, and the goodness that shines from the person's general aura will also encourage goodwill.

Our ancestors called this, "deok (virtue)" or a person's character. Innate leadership strengthens a person's character and or personality, and this denotes strength of character as well. A person who has "deok," will never break down.

Is Jesus Christ great because he was Hercules in disguise? Is Confucius famous throughout the world only because he was a great scholar?

I do not expect as much from you children. Just be aware that honesty is a virtue and it will strengthen your willpower. It is the best of all virtues.

The Beautiful Virtues vs. Sinful Deeds

The winner will give up his body as a sacrifice, while the loser will do the same with his tongue. The winner will show the truth of his words via actions, while the loser will use words to argue why he acted in a certain way. A winner will take up an attitude of responsibility, while the loser will always break promises. The winner will avoid punishment by acting properly, and will then receive his just reward, while the loser will come up with all sorts of intrigues to win the prize and receive his just punishment. The winner will serve the people and earn a title, while the loser will thirst after a title and run into trouble.

When the winner makes a mistake, he will say, "I have sinned," while the loser will say, "I have sinned because of you." The winner will issue forth truths, while the loser will have all sorts of excuses. The winner will make clear the difference between "yes" and "no," while the loser will say just enough to support his claim. To the winner, the day will be twenty-five hours long, while for the loser, the day will be twenty-three days long. The winner will work hard and play hard and rest hard. The loser will dilly-dally in work, play, and rest. The winner will allocate his schedule as necessary, while the loser will be at the mercy of Time. The winner will not fear losing, while the loser will fear even winning. The winner will live for the process, while the loser will live for the results. The winner will see the sun above the clouds, while the loser will see the rain hidden in the clouds.

The winner will know the bittersweet happiness of rising after a fall, while the loser will curse his bad luck after a fall. The winner will make a path through the snow, for when there is a will, there is a way, while the loser will wait for the snow to melt. The winner will stand before an audience on stage, while the loser will stay in the stands. The winner will use failures as a mirror, while the loser will toss his success into the wastebasket, like throwing away a tissue. The winner will hoist the sail when he sees the wind rise, while the loser will see the wind rising and lower the sail from the mast. The winner will have good control over money, while the loser will be ruled by money. The winner will have dreams in his pocket, while the loser will have only greed in his pockets. The winner will say, "Let's try again," while the loser will say "There is no use in trying again." The winner will be a "brave sinner," while the loser will be a "cowardly winner." The winner will believe in sweating for the win (hard work), while the loser will believe in luck. The winner will rise with the sun, while the loser will wait for the sun to rise. The winner will fall seven times and rise eight times, while the loser will curse falling seven times. The winner will calculate while running, while the loser will be calculating even before starting to run. The winner will listen carefully, while the loser will only wait for his turn to speak. The winner will be natural, while the loser will be a braggart. The winner will seek another road. The loser will think that there is only one road.

The winner will respect someone with talents that surpass him, while the loser will be jealous and try to find a hole in his armor. The winner will befriend those of a lesser station, while the loser will try to boss them around. The winner will race regardless of the prize or the status to be won, while the loser will race only for the prize. The winner will seek the meaning even when he becomes the last, while the loser will only see meaning when he places first. The winner will find happiness in the process. The loser will only see happiness when he has finished. (From the Jewish *Torah.*•)

The road where one learns the virtues is the path to goodness, while the road to dishonesty is rife with real failures.

To learn is to make one's own. And this means that this in itself is a virtue. The rest is meaningless.

To know the right way to behave is not the be-all and end-all. The will to do what is right, and the conviction to do so will bolster you.

When the Puritans•• espoused Stoicism, they upheld the rules and were hard on themselves, and they trained hard. These values will serve you well even by today's standards.

Children, can you sense that there are good virtues that we should emulate? Then all I ask of you is that you learn both good and evil.

Among them, there is one in particular that you should think about. That is "responsibility." You must learn responsibility with both mind and body.

Responsibility as a student, as a daughter, as a subordinate, as a boss,

• I would like to start with an excerpt from the Jewish *Torah*. The excerpt refers to the "diaspora," the Jewish people living abroad away from their homeland of Israel, and those who scattered across the four corners of the Earth, but still kept some aspects of their Jewish culture.

•• The Puritans are a sector of Christians who believed in asceticism and stoicism. They turned away from greed and followed the natural order of things.

responsibility towards work… and responsibility as a human being that has been blessed with the gift of Life.

When I talk about "responsibility," I mean that you must come upon this realization yourself and put it into action. If everyone fulfills his personal calling or destiny, then nothing will go amiss in this world.

The reason why this world is so full of strife is because we do not take up the mantle of responsibility and choose instead to blame others.

In *The Analects of Confucius*, the ancient Chinese theologian mentions responsibility as one of the highest of virtues. For a king must act like a king, and a vassal like a vassal, and a father as a father, and a son as a son.

Be Religious

Hyo Jung, in this world, I find that in my point of view, the most frustrating of people ask about the existence of God. This is akin to foolishly asking, "Do I have a father?" If we didn't have a father, then how did we come into this world?

As my existence confirms the existence of my father, all things in this world follow a natural order, and the behavior of the universe confirms the existence of God or an all-knowing, omnipresent and omnipotent deity.

The important thing to note is that we believe in an all-knowing God because He exists. We do not believe in God's existence solely because of our selfish desire to go to Heaven, but rather, this attitude must persist regardless of whether He exists or not. Because in this life, the world we live in is important, and living with purpose is important in and of itself. We must not be too selfish in asking for wishes to be granted by God, and if we only believe in God because of the promised gift of eternal life in Heaven, then isn't this looking for a gift horse in the mouth?

Faith must be unconditional. This is similar to taking up what I referred to as taking up the mantle of responsibility. That a person must act with humility before a greater Being, with some trepidation, to be sure. This is the right attitude to adopt before our Creator, and we must follow His will with thankfulness. It's worth living a meaningful life, and we must still be humble…this is what I would define as faith.

One of the highest virtues that one can adopt as a human is humility. If a person is humble, then he will naturally love God.

St. Augustine also said that we believe because we wish to know, not because we wish to believe in order to know.

Hae-June, young people these days sometimes misuse their reason to bolster their arguments, and they refuse to believe otherwise. My generation was also guilty of this.

When I was young and in love with Grandma, my first assignment was as a second lieutenant, the 12th Infantry Division, in the South Korean Army. I had just graduated from Korea Military Academy and was assigned to a small village somewhere in Gangwon Province.

First-line troops normally do not have days off. To meet Grandma, I had to come up with all sorts of reasons why I needed a day off, and I was granted my request only every couple of months. It was for one day only. How precious was this single day in Seoul to meet my beloved!

But alas. One of these precious nights was spent with someone I will call "crazy man." He was a friend from the barracks. I spent the whole night arguing with him over the non-existence of God.

The reason why I call this friend "crazy man," is not because he really was crazy. He once wrote a short story titled, "Crazy Man," during his senior year at Korea Military Academy that was nothing short of astonishing. This friend of mine came from a good family that was also very religious starting from his grandfather's adoption of Buddhism.

That night, my friend lost his argument. I, as a very stubborn fellow kept on saying God didn't exist (I was secretly an atheist back then). It's true that a stupid person is brave and foolhardy. When I think back upon this, I am ashamed of my former self.

The truth is, atheism is even stronger than religion.

If there is no God, then why even deny His existence. And how could He die when he didn't even exist?

The reason I started to believe in God is all because of Grandma. Grandma was a student at Ewha Womans University back then, and she had received her first communion quite early.

I was a country bumpkin from the city of Daegu, and I was an ignorant fool in terms of theology. But in order to win over Grandma, in 1960, when I was stationed at Fort Sill,• I received a baptism from a minister surnamed Hamilton.

When I finally confessed my love for Grandma, I used a metaphor regarding God. It was slightly blasphemous.

I couldn't actually utter the words, "I love you." So I improvised and said, "Dear Sook, if Rocky loves God then it's because you exist."

I too have had my sentimental moments. Isn't it funny?

• The Fort Sill Military Reservation is in Oklahoma, USA. It was established in 1869 by a Major General named Phillip H. Sheridan. The original reservation was called Wichita, but Sheridan named it after a former friend who was killed in action. Today, it also has a military hospital on its base.

Children, as you should never ask, "What is life," likewise, you should never debate over God's existence. To have faith is to believe with some suspension of rational thought. Faith surpasses human logic, and when we have reconciled this with the wonders of the God-ruled universe, we will have achieved what the Buddhists commonly refer to as "nirvana."

To have faith is to humbly submit to God Almighty, and harkens back to what I said about taking up the mantle of responsibility.

I coolly dismiss those who aren't humble. I have no respect for them. Then you should realize that I will never accept a new member of the family who is an atheist.

Chapter 3

On Scholarship

The Road to Becoming a Scholar

The Donkey That Carries Books on His Back

Respect Your Mentors

"A Day's Morning Does Not Come Twice"

Beware of Those Who Only Read One Book

To Succeed in Entrance Exams

The Road to Becoming a Scholar

Confucius said that the road to scholarship will only be open to those who polish their hearts and transform from a novice to a master. Without this, one cannot know the truth, and if one does not know the truth, then there are no roads. There are two reasons why scholarship is also important. It's so that a person acts like a person, and can then turn their minds towards the mysteries of the universe.

I need not say more, but without scholarship for mankind, I dare say that we would still be wandering around in the dark. Without scholarship, we would be mere animals.

From ancient times, they have called humans "the lord of all things," but without scholarship, we would be indistinguishable from beasts.

A mere cow or a pig does not have a history; therefore, mankind, without history and scholarship, would still be surrounded by darkness.

Man's rational mind twinkles even brighter than the first star at dawn. Science, at best, takes the natural order of the universe too seriously, and overflowing wealth should both be attributed to scholarship and man's mastery of it.

We are not born with scholarships. But we learn as soon as we are out of the womb. We learn to clap our baby hands together in glee. And as soon as we start attending school, we embark on a life where the pursuit of knowledge will stay with us until our dying day.

One of the problems is that people do not enjoy studying. When I was young, Grandpa really hated going to school, to the extent that I would make up all sorts of excuses then become really recalcitrant when I did have to eventually go.

When I did not have a valid excuse, I would say I was already late, then I would throw a temper tantrum with tears rolling down my face.

My mother would say to me, "It's not even eight o'clock in the morning. What on Earth are you talking about?" Then I would say, "But the sun is high in the sky…it is really high…" and keep on refusing to go.

Even before her death, my mother would often retell this anecdote with great amusement to all who would listen. She would affectionately call her youngest, me, "the cranky child who refused to go to school as soon as the sun rose."

"No matter how brilliant, if you do not learn, then realization will be beyond you." So said Mencius.• To him, in order to live as a human being, studying and learning were paramount. A person who is a professional maker of jade beads must study how to form perfect circles by grinding the jade carefully.

In one of Chu Hsi's works, it says:

"A boy can easily become old,
And scholarship be beyond reach.
Even if you have limited time,
Do not listen to this lightly.

• Mencius (BC 372–BC 289) was a Chinese philosopher who advanced some of the teachings of his predecessor, Confucius, and played an important role in talking about the four virtues: benevolence, righteousness, propriety, and wisdom. These four virtues, he would claim, create and define Man.

The spring grass near the pond
Are still slumbering and have not yet awakened.
How the leaves whisper of autumn as they rustle in the wind."

I would like to reiterate the importance of learning, and as Confucius said before, "The person who studies cannot surpass one who enjoys studying, and a person who likes to learn cannot surpass one who loves to learn."

To paraphrase Shakespeare, "Knowledge is what gives us wings. Without the pursuit of knowledge, then a man must crawl on the ground." Even Goethe said once, "Great happiness comes from the pursuit of knowledge."

But the troubling part is that in order to learn best, you must make learning very appealing. But how to go about it? They don't say.

So I ask you now, "How can you make learning fun?"

It must come through constant inquiry and self-reflection.

Zhuge Liang said to his son, "With a quiet sense of self-reflection, purify yourself, then with modesty, increase your knowledge through study. If you are immodest, then your selfishness will grow and skirt the way of the Truth, and if you are not calm and holy, then the road ahead will look arduous. Scholarship will come through careful study and reflection."

Zhuge Liang tries to teach us the modest way of learning, not for self-gain but to reach a higher self, and also says that modesty in all things may pave the way towards learning. This may be a brilliant adage, but I say, it is difficult to put into practice.

So how to cultivate the mind? First, ask yourself when you are the happiest. This happens when the outcome is good but the process is difficult, or when you have succeeded.

The reason why we scale the mountain is to feel the rush of adrenaline as we shout from the mountaintop and admire the vista below.

If you are a mountaineer, then you will know that as you scale every hill, as you find it difficult to breathe during a steep ascent and feel like your breath may leave your body. We may even say to ourselves, "Today is the last day I will climb the mountain."

But a few days later, we find ourselves putting on our mountain gear again, ending with the proper footwear.

Why? From the apex, you feel great, and you feel accomplished, and you feel larger than life. You cannot find this unique feeling elsewhere.

Can't we apply this to studying? Studying is difficult and particular. This is why sometimes we don't want to study.

Studying is dissimilar to scaling a mountain, in the sense that it doesn't give you a reward right away…unless it's an entrance examination or a different type of test that they administer for job seekers.

Then what?

It all depends on your mindset. You may not understand it now, but try anyway, as Grandpa recommends here.

When your day's activities are done and you are lying in bed, close your eyes and breathe in and out three times. While doing so, repeat this phrase: "I love God and Father and Mother and Teacher and my friends. I wish to work for all of my loved ones. In order to do so, I will always be healthy and pretty and study hard."

After repeating this mantra with your eyes closed, breathe in and out three times, then imagine yourself studying. Then say to yourself: "I take enjoyment in studying. I enjoy studying. I enjoy studying the most." Repeat this out loud. Say this with all sincerity. You will be able to persuade yourself once you do this.

My teachings are not the law. I ask only this, that you try it.

The Donkey That Carries Books on His Back

On the East Coast of the United States, there was an old man who operated a hot dog restaurant near a church, some distance away from the city. The old man's hot dogs were famous for their taste, even hundreds of miles away.

On the roof of the hot dog establishment stood the sign: "The most delicious hot dogs in America." Everyone, it seemed, appeared to visit the hot dog stand to taste the delicious street food. The old man would greet the visitors at the entrance with a wide smile.

"Don't just buy one. Buy two. They're really delicious."

The visitors would taste the never-before-seen hot dog buns, toasted to perfection and crispy, with pickles, and onions and mustard creating an even more delicious symphony in the mouth.

The hard-working young women working there please the customers. They would lick their lips and say to themselves, "That a hot dog could taste so delicious," as they strode away from the shop.

The old man would wave at them and say, "Please visit again. This helps me do business, and the ones who work here for me earn money for college."

So many repeat customers visit the old man's hot dog stand, over and over.

One day, the old man's son, who had a Ph.D. from Harvard University, visited him. He viewed the man's business, then said, to him:

"Father, how can you do business like this in a downturn economy such as this? You must downsize right away. First off, you must fire four and keep only two of your waitresses. Stop greeting the customers at the door. Prepare the hot dogs instead. Buy cheaper buns and sausages from your middleman. The mustard and the pickles too, buy them for cheap, and do away with the onions. Do you understand what I'm saying?"

The old man was proud of his son. He was so grateful.

"Of course. My son, with a Ph.D. He's different." He did not waste any time in putting his son's advice to good use.

He lowered the sign and stayed in the kitchen where he only used cheap ingredients. He only kept one waitress, to do his bidding.

About three months later, the old man's son came to him.

"Father, how is the business?" he asked him.

The old man's shoulders slumped. He pointed to the empty parking lot.

The parking lot, which had once been crowded with many cars, stood empty with a few stray leaves blowing about.

"As you have said, it's a terrible recession."

This is a true story that I came across accidentally while reading.

In the *Talmud*, it says, "There are some scholars that are similar to donkeys. They are the ones who carry books only." What a frightening thought.

That is why Confucius, in his *Analects*, says, "If you do not contemplate what you study, then it is dark, and if you do not speculate while learning then you are in grave danger." Even Mencius says, "If you only believe in books, then it is the same as not having books." He warns us of this phenomenon.

In the hot dog restaurant example, the lesson to be learned is that there is a limitation to book learning. There is a trap within it. To learn is to systematically learn something that someone else has learned. That is why if you only learn, without inserting your own point of view, then you may be in danger.

Think while you learn. This is the way towards real knowledge.

A humble and modest stance is important as you learn from books. The Harvard Business School graduate is humbled before the real world, wouldn't you say?

Without meditation, knowledge gleaned from books is useless, and without a humble mindset, scholarship may lead to ruination.

In the *Sohak*, which was written during the Song Dynasty, a person named Chengyichuan once said:

"There are three things that will cause distress for man. First, the passing of the highest-level state exam after boyhood, second, rising to a good government post thanks to father's connections, then third, writing well thanks to superb talent." If you believe only in your talent and start studying, then you are being foolish.

Does it not also say in *The Analects of Confucius* that you must say, "true knowledge is acknowledging what you know and don't know." How humbling is this tale?

"If three people are walking together then within their ranks there is my teacher," according to *The Analects*.

Jacque Rousseau also said something similar. "There are three teachers for Man. The first is Nature, the second is man, and the third is all things."

Children, there is another I must warn you about. In order to become a true scholar, then your learning must bear fruit.

How can learning bear fruit? It is through action. If thought isn't moved to action, then we are all donkeys carrying books.

Thomas Huxley• once said, "Life's great achievement is not in book learning but in action."

That is why Francis Bacon,•• a great scholar himself, supported this claim as well. "Those who put to use their learning are the wisest of men. Scholars do not teach the practice of how. Using knowledge gleaned from books is wisdom above mere studies."

Jesus Christ and Confucius did not say much about a person's words, but rather, his actions. They taught through actions, rather than words (there are those that may disagree with me). Dare I say, that their students and their followers may have just summarized his actions via words.

There is a word in Korean, called "poongsin." This is a difficult phrase. Initially, it was "poongchae," but basically it means to do with one's body. Generally speaking, it means that Jesus Christ and Confucius, and other saints taught through their actions.

It is easy to preach. It is not so easy to do with one's body.

In ancient times, there was a saying, "Learn from all, ask precisely, think deeply, distinguish clearly, and act sincerely."••• Without action, knowledge is useless and is like a tree that doesn't bear fruit.

"A scholar who doesn't act is similar to a cloud that doesn't rain." This is an adage from the East.

• Thomas H. Huxley (1825–1895) was a British biologist and anthropologist who supported Darwin's theory of evolution.

•• Francis Bacon (1561–1626) was a British politician and philosopher who has also been called "the father of empiricism." Empiricism can also be distilled simply into the scientific method.

••• A book of the ancient Chinese philosophies, *The Doctrine of the Mean* emphasizes practicing the art of not too much and not too little.

Respect Your Mentors

In the East, there was a saying that can be summarized thusly: "Respect your Teacher as your King and your Parents." It was even a virtue for pupils not supposed to step on the shadows of their teachers. This is a beautiful example of East Asian morality.

Sometimes, I hear every now and then that a teacher has been beaten by his students. This hurts my heart.

The reason why I decided to write this book is in part due to these terrible actions. "This simply cannot be done. I have to start by teaching our children."

The *Zīzhi Tōngjiàn*• is an old history book and in it, you can easily find a scholar of Confucian classics, but it is difficult to find a real mentor. It is not easy to find such a scholar, no matter how far and wide you search. It would be best if the teachers we had were all brilliant and outstanding, but this is not always the case.

The problem is that a teacher is a teacher regardless of whether he has merit or not. You must respect the teacher because he is the teacher. This attitude is the correct one. This is similar to how I receive love from my dear grandchildren, for I am your Grandfather.

In order to make this world a better one, it would be best to say, "We like because he is here, and we respect him because we have to follow." It is not always, alas, "We follow him because we like him, and we respect him because he's an outstanding gentleman." The first attitude is sometimes the one that we have to adopt. This is what keeps the order

• The history book is from the North Song Dynasty and lists historical events in chronological order.

by respecting authority.

In the *Talmud*, it says, "If your father and teacher are on one boat and it starts sinking, you must save the teacher first."

In the East, we think the opposite. But the Jewish people, even during ancient times, held their teachers in great respect. Do you think they did not respect their fathers as well? Of course, they did. But this is their teaching and their law, and what has upheld their Jewish traditions to date.

While great teachers may be rare in today's world and age, if you look hard enough, there are some splendid ones. The reason why teachers are important is not just because they are needed during the school year. Their importance transcends graduation.

Upon graduating, you will leave the world of systematic learning. This is why you need your former teacher.

When you start working, you should make an effort to visit your old teachers and get some advice, both on scholarly things and even for work. This shouldn't take you too long. Two or three teachers are all you need. You need to take up the role of receiving counseling from your former teachers, rather than learning from them as you once did in school.

When you are seeking guidance and advice, even if your teacher or teachers are incapable of finding a correct answer, it is good for you to communicate with them. The important thing is that you are there, honoring them and seeking their advice.

At times, your teacher's advice may seem foolhardy. This is only natural. You are in the real world, and he is in the ivory tower. You outpace him by having more information and knowledge. But as I have reiterated over and over, the important thing is that you are seeking his advice anyway.

When you have a problem that doesn't go away, you sometimes seek the advice of others. But what is this? During this process, sometimes you arrive at a solution by yourself. Wouldn't this be grand if a solution came to you as you were consulting your beloved teacher?

You should seek out your teacher at other times too. This act in itself lends itself to propriety and your respect for the pecking order. This is very human of us.

Once you put this advice to good use, you will realize, "a teacher is actually really different."

"A Day's Morning Does Not Come Twice"

In India, there is an adage that says, "Spend your days wisely, so that in your slumbers at night you can rest easy. And spend your youth wisely, so that in your old age, you may be comfortable."

As with everything, timing is of the utmost importance. If you don't study when you should, then you will suffer…seemingly forever. These days, the school system is very rigid and structured, so if you do not advance up a grade when you should, then you will run into trouble.

If you don't understand math during elementary school and then advance up to middle school anyway, then you will not be able to keep up. The aftereffect of this will be that you will be frightened of studying, not just mathematics but all subjects. You will fall behind in all your classes, fail a grade, then lose all interest in studying. You will inevitably fail your thesis. This is why you have to keep up, especially in the sciences. The sciences need a strong foundation and as you advance up, you may need to refer back to the basics, so this is of the utmost importance.

Mathematics and English are similar. I am reiterating the necessity of doing well in mathematics. As you advance up another level, you must keep up. About 90 percent of students hate math, but if you understand the basics then make it more difficult, there is nothing more delightful and fun like math. If you spend enough time when you should on math, you will spend less time reviewing and catching up, and it will be a boon to you during entrance examinations. While everyone else is stressing over math, you will be able to tackle other subjects with ease.

They may say math isn't really important in the real world, but in my view, these people are foolish. Mathematics teaches us logical thinking and precision. Beauty and inspiration are also found here.

In work, speaking more foreign languages is of the utmost importance. During your school days, you should study at least two. If you cannot, due to extenuating circumstances, then you should at least speak English well. Speaking a foreign language with ease and fluency wields as much power as cash in today's society.

So which wins? Preparation or revision? There are many theories and pundits on this subject, but I say, it depends on the subject. Most of the sciences require preparation before the subject is studied in school while for the humanities and statistics, revision is better. Mathematics is not about just mere memorization, so please prepare before classes. I mean it.

The one who studies the most is the one who wins at the end. It's good to solve math problems that you know how to solve, and it is good to memorize English phrases. You cannot win over someone like this. This is the power of revision.

If you really want to do well in everything, then repetition, even for things you know how to do well, will turn you into an expert. This is why I mean by the power of revision.

Some minor points I have to make here. Some dangers lie ahead for you. When you study, don't use an eraser. Just strike it out with a pencil. Strike it out once, where you have made a mistake, so that you will remember why and what you did wrong.

There are geniuses that do not need a notebook, but for you children, I think a notebook is necessary.

Why? Long words aren't necessary. This is because of entrance examinations and a societal flaw. You must learn how to cleanly and precisely write documents, and you must start early with notebooks.

You must write legibly as well. This is practice. For calculations, do not be hasty. I'm warning you.

An old Western adage says, "To the foolish, old age will be winter, but to the wise man, it will be the golden years of his life." There may be exceptions, but the distinguishing factor between the foolish and the wise man may be in his schoolboy years and how much (or how little) he studied.

"The perennial years of youth do not return, and a day's morning does not come twice. At every moment, work to the best of your ability. Time waits for no man." This is according to Tao Yuanming• in one of his poems.

• Tao Yuanming (365–427) was a Chinese poet from the Qin Dynasty. He wrote and sang many poems regarding Nature's Beauty.

Zhuge Liang,[•] later a regent of Shu Han, during the Three Kingdoms Period of China, said this to his son:

"If you are negligent, then you will never plumb the depths of beauty in scholarship, and if you are hasty and imprudent, then you will be unable to be a man of good character. Time passes quickly unbeknownst to you, and as you age, you will lose the timing, then lose your will. Time will see you shed leaves like an old tree, and you will fall into extreme poverty while bemoaning your cursed fate in some dilapidated house somewhere, and you will be beyond helping."

In other words, a person's entire life may be just a blink of an eye, for it passes that quickly. And important, crucial moments may be just once or twice in one's lifetime. The time is now, to take up the mantle of responsibility and respond to these crucial moments that may come to you without a moment's notice.

One of these crucial moments is during your school days. You will have to work even harder in the real world, but during your school days, one sincere, large effort will suffice. Do not while away your days when you are young, and study hard.

If you do not wish to spend your life in Winter, and if you wish for your older years to not be like a shedding tree, then greet the day at dawn and spend your days wisely while you are younger.

A morning does not return twice.

• Zhuge Liang (181–234) was a Chinese statesman, military engineer, strategist, and writer. He was the father of Zhuge Zhan, a Chinese military general and politician in Shu Han.

Beware of Those Who Only Read One Book

A person must read books; this is a given. The problem is that there are far too many to read. Then what kind of book should you read?

A man named Max Weber• once said, "A book that is not worth reading twice is not even worth reading once." So what does he mean by this? How can you tell if a book will be worth reading twice?

Ralph Waldo Emerson•• said, "I do not read books that are less than a year old." This means that you should read old books. The classics are what he is referring to.

The older the book is, the better. If a book has been in print for over a thousand years, then how brilliant and wise must it be, that people are still reading it to this day!

There are many old books, and many of them are good. That is why Grandpa has compiled a list of "books to read" in this book's appendix. I used statistical analysis to select the books, with data collected from several different organizations (I used mode). For Korean books, you can select your reading material from new bestsellers and books recommended by your teachers.

I know of a successful American businessman who said to his son that he has lived many times over through reading. He was bragging, of course.

• Max Weber (1864–1920) was a German sociologist and political economist whose ideas "profoundly influenced social theory and research." Among his written works are, *The Protestant ethic and the Spirit of Capitalism*, which traverses the link between Protestantism and capitalism, and social action theory, which says that people are too concerned with efficiency in the modern era and are ignoring ethics and tradition, which, he argued, causes enormous social problems.

•• Ralph Waldo Emerson (1803–1882) was an American essayist and philosopher who participated in the transcendentalist movement in history. "Intuition" is the only way to understand reality, according to Emerson. He drew largely from British and German Romanticism.

"Beware of any man who has only read one book," says Benjamin Disraeli.• I say, don't be wary of him, but do not make him your teacher.

To Succeed in Entrance Exams

Hyo Sung and Hae-Yeon, an entrance exam usually doesn't have much to do with your studies. Unfortunately, in order to be on "the list," you have to take them. I feel heartbroken for young women, who spend too much time studying.

There is something wrong with the admissions process, but no real-world case can evade it. That is why don't fault the process, but think of ways to replace it.

It is a test that cannot be evaded. It is an arduous task ahead of you, but you must try anyway.

You will be frightened. It will be the first big competition of your life. You will be worried. Because it is a bloody one.

It is a fight that you cannot avoid. It is a challenge to be met. You have to face it full on. This is what they call, "taking the bull by the horns." You must work really hard so that you have more experience than others. This will ensure you a place on "the list."

The answer lies in how you study. Time is fair to all. Every student studies hard. But this won't suffice. Something has to set you apart from the rest.

• Benjamin Disraeli (1804–1881) was a British politician who served as Prime Minister twice. He was a member of the Conservative Party of England. He staunchly defended imperialism and colonialism, a driving force of the British Empire during the Victorian era. He is the writer of books such as *Coningsby*, a political satire.

How? And what?

The first is concentration. Gather your heart and mind. You have to increase your concentration.

How can you concentrate while studying?

It should be fun. But studying isn't always fun.

Then what to do? It's not easy.

But there is a way.

Hyo Sung and Hae-Yeon! Pay attention!

Before studying, sit in front of your desk and close your eyes. Slowly breathe in and out three times. The breath here should be from the belly (I will explain what this is in the next chapter). Then raise your right arm to shoulder level. Then give a thumbs up. Then open your eyes and observe your thumb. Then imagine yourself happily studying. Then shout, "I am studying happily. I can succeed at any exam." Then close your eyes then visualize yourself happily studying. Then you will feel your arm becoming heavy. Then slowly, very slowly, lower your arm. This should be done effortlessly. When your arm has reached your knee, then your head will be clear. Then you can start studying quietly.

If your heart feels heavy for some reason, or you feel worries gnawing at you, breathe in and out two or three times, then visualize a still lake. A lake that is as clear as glass, where the wind gently blows, causing ripples. Then your heart will become calm. Then say out loud, "One, two, three," then open your eyes again. Then commence with your studies for that day.

This should take you no longer than five minutes.

This is very effective. After a month or two, you will be able to focus just by breathing through the belly two or three times. Do not forgo this step, no matter what day of the week it is. Like I said, this will be enormously effective.

Secondly, in order to concentrate, there should be a change. No matter how important a test is, you cannot study twelve months out of the year. You should take walks, play tennis, and listen to music. I hope you listen to my advice.

Why do we need a change?

This is an old story, but an American professor once conducted a study that I will detail for you now. He gathered a few people in a room, had them lie down, then did not allow them to see anything new, hear anything new, and prevented them from touching anything for five days. Over half could not make it past two days, but there were a few who survived.

After the test was over, the researchers conducted a cognition test. All study participants experienced a decrease in cognition. Not only this, but a line looked curved and skewed to them, and they could not distinguish between something that was close and something that was far off in the distance. The world seemed to spin, and some hallucinated.

The conclusion to be drawn from this? In order to retain consciousness and concentration, one must continually introduce changes.

So what kind of change can you give? This is why I suggested playing tennis and listening to music.

What if you feel pressed for time? You may think you don't even have enough hours in a day to study. But as the study showed, you need new stimuli, otherwise you will not succeed. According to psychologists, an average person's ability to concentrate does not exceed three minutes.

Studying for an exam should take about a year if time is limited, but it should not exceed three years. It's a long battle. If you study the same way for a year, do you think that your willpower and nerves will stay put? No. Even if you are able to endure it for a year, your output and effectiveness will decrease.

If one doesn't concentrate, then it is useless, whether or not he sits at the desk for twelve months out of the whole year. They say, someone is smart or has a good memory, but I say that rather than the person being smart, I bet anything that he's better at concentrating than most people. That is why I believe that the be-all and end-all for whether a person is successful in studying lies in how well he "concentrates." That is why stimuli were removed in the preceding experiment that I outlined earlier. That is why we need to play tennis and take walks, to introduce changes.

So should we play tennis for hours every day? No. We are playing to do well in exams, and listening to music in order to do well in our studies. I stress moderation in all things.

Listen closely, Hae-June and Hyo Jung.

When you start studying, take a break every thirty minutes from your desk. For about thirty seconds, stretch your arms and draw a wide circle. Shake your arms and your head. When you're at the two-hour mark, walk in your room for about five minutes. Move your body. Move your neck and do some stretching exercises.

Turn on music. Music that you like, of course. While you listen to music that you like, pace in your room. Gaze out the window at the blue skies outside. Breathe deep, from your belly. Then your body, which may have gotten heavy during your studies, will feel refreshed, and you will feel lighter too.

On the weekends, you should reserve an hour for exercise. This is why I recommend tennis. If you are unable to play tennis for various reasons, then you can take a walk. The reason why I recommend playing tennis and taking a walk is because they are linked to an increase in brain activity. Have your father accompany you when you play tennis or take a walk.

For the men of our family! Take heed, that spending time with your children and playing sports is more important than playing golf!

I am going to give you a real-life example of why it's beneficial to spend time exercising with your father during your youth.

Several years ago, one of my high-ranking subordinate's sons was admitted, early decision, to Seoul National University. According to him, on the weekends, he would take his son and play tennis for an hour, and go to church with him on Sundays.

To subtract about three hours from the whole week for church and exercise! But the son had done well and gained early acceptance to SNU. Like I said, it's not the hours you put in at your desk, but the quality of them. This is why "concentration" is important.

There is another way you can introduce change. Once a month, study with a friend. You can check each other while studying for an important subject or a tricky one, and review together. This will introduce change, and you will do better in exams. You will also be able to see how your friend excels in a particular area. This is an added plus.

Chapter 4

On Training Your Body

Health Comes First

A person, first and foremost, needs to be healthy. Health comes first, and studies come second. All blessings stem from this. You must be healthy in order to help others; otherwise, you will only harm them.

To be healthy? I am referring to the health of the mind and of the heart. If you have a healthy mind, then you will conquer all sorts of illnesses. That is why you must always be in good health.

Then how to tell if one is healthy, in both mind and soul?

We refer to Romans 12:2, which says, "Do not conform to the patterns of this world, but be transformed by the renewing of your mind." An American doctor gave this Bible verse as a prescription to many patients, in lieu of medicine.

"About 70 percent of patients who came to me only had illnesses that stemmed from habits," he said.

That is why instead of prescribing medications, he wrote, "Be transformed by the renewing of your mind." But most patients actually thanked him for curing them with this verse.

Hae-June, Hyo Jung, the fact of the matter is, this should not come as a surprise and the doctor is not bluffing. This is real and the most effective of prescriptions.

Why? There will be no end to a full explanation, so I shall give you a simple one.

Our bodies are controlled by our minds, as you should already be aware of. The mind can be described as the conscious mind and the unconscious mind. Most people believe our lives are controlled by the conscious mind, but the unconscious mind exerts a greater influence.

That is why if you are feeling unwell, if you consciously say you are not sick, then the unconscious mind will kick in and most ailments will disappear, like a lie.

Isn't this unbelievable? But if you do as Grandpa says, with all sincerity, then you will find that it has a high degree of veracity to it.

To put it simply, our health can be maintained by tapping into the unconscious, and small ailments can be cured by the unconscious mind. This is not just my own personal belief but something that modern-day psychologists have come up with, and the previous true story of the American doctor shows that it does have implications in the real world.

A Western proverb says, "When a person dies, his body is eaten away by maggots, and while he is alive, he is slowly eaten away by his anxiety and worries."

Our bodies are worn down by worries and the start of diseases is due to extreme anxiety and worries. That is why jealousy, fear, and anxiety, along with worrying, can damage our nervous systems and endocrine glands.

One of our greatest fears, cancer, has roots in stress. How insightful, therefore, is the adage, "renew your minds."

Children, I say this often, but just follow my lead without asking too many questions. Just trust and believe what I say.

First, always be joyful in your heart. I believe that health is a result of habits and is just as important as Fate. They also say that personality is Fate, but habits and Fate are also results of your personality. That is why good habits will create good health, and will be the first step towards it, and likewise, you should always be grateful and think joyful thoughts, and see that the glass is half full in every circumstance.

In the *Talmud*, it says, "If you lose a foot, be grateful that you have not lost both, and if you have lost both, then be thankful for your intact throat."

How direct is this approach. Even in the face of tragedy, it shows bravery and a positive attitude. Then you will not despair.

Secondly, you should love others. When you love, endorphins are released at their greatest rate.

In the *Book of Filial Daughter Simcheong*, there is an absurdist story about a blind man who regains his sight. They all thought Simcheong must have died, but they met her again. How many endorphins must have been released! No wonder why her father regained his vision.

Thirdly, always pray. With all your heart and all your might. Thank the bright dawn, the joy of today, and be thankful for your health.

As you grow older, you will experience the miracle of prayer. In the universe, prayer is the way we humbly meet the greatest Being, Our Heavenly Father.

When you think about this, it truly is a scary idea. With this fearful heart, be sincere, be thankful for everything, and pray. Most health problems can be resolved with prayer.

Fourth, close your eyes and meditate. As many times as you can throughout the day, as time allows. Close your eyes, relax your body, and practice "breathing deep from the abdomen." As you catch your breath, meditate.

Think upon your last vacation spot, the beautiful East Sea and Mount Seorak's beautiful vistas, or imagine yourself happily smiling and in good health. If you cannot do any of the above, and everything feels like a burden to you, empty your mind and your heart. The latter is not easy. That is why it's better to think about good things.

You can sit in a chair, or lie down, or even stand while meditating. As time and circumstances allow, of course. Keep it within five minutes and the more times you practice meditation, the better.

"Breathing deep from your abdomen" is just as important as meditation. Humans are actually supposed to breathe from the belly, and not the chest. As the environment grew more complex, our breathing changed from emerging from deep within our bellies to our chests instead. You can see babies breathing from their bellies.

According to evolutionists we humans, before we became homo sapiens' predecessor, homo erectus, used to crawl on all fours, and we practiced breathing from the abdomen back then. That is why people who struggle with this type of breathing may have some luck when they lie on their stomachs and try again. This may have some truth to it.

As a military cadet at Korea Military Academy, when I used to play rugby, there were times when I was so out of breath that I could barely stand it. Then the coaches used to tell us to put our arms on our knees and lie face down. When I did this, I could recover my breath. The coaches did not know the origins of this method and only knew it from experience.

Why is breathing deeply from the belly so great? It's excellent for getting rid of tiredness. Why? Physiologically speaking, if you do this, your diaphragm rises and falls and increases your lung capacity, allowing for increased oxygen supply. In modern-day experiments, breathing from the abdomen allows for about twice the oxygen supply as that of shallow breathing from the chest.

Fifthly, eat a variety of foods for a balanced diet. Some examples include a mostly vegetarian diet, organic or natural foods, etc. There are many types of diets, with some theories and opinions on them, and they are all good.

But in my opinion, I think a balanced diet is all about portion control. Grandpa is a little bit overweight, so this may fall on deaf ears, but I think that stopping before you are full is better. This is the most important. Our family members have hearty appetites, and this constraint may be difficult, but especially after the age of forty, we have to exert self-control and bear in mind the importance of portion control.

When You Are Angry

This world is not always ruled by events fortuitous to you. Pitiful events, events that make you blow your lid, sad events…all these types of life events will present themselves before you. This is what it means to live in a human society. Out of all these feelings, you must guard against the most dangerous: anger.

Firstly, do not suppress your anger. Forget instead. When all else fails, then get good and angry. But expressing your anger has to have some wit to it.

Secondly, cry. If you are sad, cry. Cry all you want. Former U.S. President Abraham Lincoln cried. So did our great Korean admiral Yi Sun-sin. You aren't human unless you know how to cry. Some say it's shameful for men to cry, but I say it's courageous of them. The ability to shed tears is a gift from God.

Thirdly, when a big worry is gnawing at you, do not curl up into a ball but move. You may move in your room, or pace in the front yard, or even go on a hike, which is more preferable.

If limited by time and circumstance, make use of a sharp object. Sewing or sawing a tree…both are good options.

If you go hiking, go to the apex and gaze at the vista below. Breathe from your abdomen. It must be diaphragmatic breathing, which is another way to call it. As you exhale, repeat in your head, "Worries, disappear." Then gaze at the skies above you and assess whether it's a question of life and death. Out of all the worries that men and women have day by day, how many are questions of life and death?

But what if it is a matter of life and death? Then face it head-on. Even here, it should be a "take the bull by the horns" approach. "If I die, I die, and if I live, so be it." Be proactive instead of reactive.

If it's a matter of life and death, then resolve to die. About 80 to 90 percent will live. Then pray. Pray with all your might and all your heart.

Fourthly, when you are depressed, sing. If you have an instrument, it is even better, and music is solace for those who are angry or worried. It's a balm for the soul.

You may disregard the advice I give above and dismiss them as the ramblings of an old man past his prime. But this eases my heart. If you know statistics, then it won't be a big worry. Singing is also wit.

Fifthly, forgive. If you hate, the negative energy will damage you. But this is difficult. How on Earth to forgive that bastard!

Remember Romans 12:14: "Bless those who persecute you; bless and do not curse."

It all boils down to what you resolve to do. If you cannot bless, then at least, forgive. "Fine, I forgive!" You can shout it if you want.

Cultivating One's Body and Mind

Our bodies house our minds. Our minds are important but with just resolve alone, we cannot stay healthy. Minds should be trained. This is the way towards perfect health.

If you train your body, you first think of exercise. Exercising is fine. But real physical vitality comes from the harmonious interplay of many bodily systems.

The mind-body connection, the circulatory system, etc. I wonder if the harmony of all these systems results in health. The body is a curious, mysterious, and wonderful creation, and mere human knowledge has not yet plumbed all of its depths.

How to make all these systems sing in harmony?

I don't have a ready answer. But this much is clear. You cannot force it. In all things, moderation is key. Gluttony, working too hard, drinking too much, all contribute to ill health.

Moderation and a modest attitude will harmonize the mind and body, and making them move as if one with the universe.

Take exercise as a hobby, or train and develop a part of the body that is endowed with a special quality, but for health maintenance, there are other ways.

When I think back upon the national team athletes that I had the pleasure of helping train, they were all good runners, but several of them had ailments such as a bad stomach or back pain.

That is why in order to train both the mind and the body, I suggest yoga, zen meditation, or Chinese tai chi. These practices have been around for hundreds of years, a testament to how useful they are in staying healthy.

This does not mean that exercise is unnecessary. Quite the opposite.

When you exercise, the parts of the body that you train become quite developed and your lung capacity increases, and your heart becomes healthier. But it is hard on the body, and you cannot train the body and brain at the same time. This is the fault that lies in sports. That is why the best way is to do yoga or zen meditation along with exercise.

The women of our family should know how to swim, play tennis, and ski. For the males of the family, they should surpass the skills of the women, and during their school years, practice judo or rugby. I suggest hiking for both. Once every three months, go hiking.

Create Good Habits

Bad habits can create ailments with the passage of time. A person who is always hunched over, a person who crosses his or her legs, or a person who sleeps late...I can name so many bad habits besides these. These are akin to a piggy bank spilling coins out of a hole and harmful to our health.

You must try your best in order to stay healthy, but if you have bad habits into your middle age, then you are essentially inviting in bad luck. Shall I continue with some pitfalls that one should avoid?

The first is posture. Broaden your chest. This is a family motto. If you straighten your chest, then your back will be straight. When you straighten your chest, your lungs and heart will work better, and because your back is straight, the spine will be straight as well. Isn't it a sight to behold? It also denotes confidence, courage, and purity. It's like killing three birds with one stone.

Grandpa graduated from Korea Military Academy in 1958. Two hundred and fifty enrolled, and 170 were commissioned. Among them, less than thirty became generals. But when I think back upon it, other than the generals, there was not a man among them who was sticking his chest out. One of my closest friends had excellent posture and became a three-star general. That is why posture impacts both health and inner ability; how strange.

The next is walking. Walk with confidence and a bounce to your step. You should broaden your chest and walk, with every pace a little bit longer than most people. Walk quickly. I do not need to explain further. You will see it when you try it.

Those who live in South Jeolla Province, all know of this true tale. I had it recounted to me by someone who had already passed.

One day a perfect stranger came along and asked him for a loan. He obviously refused. But when he saw the stranger walking out of the front gates, he saw that he was walking erect, with his shoulders down and chest out. He stopped the stranger and agreed to loan him the money. The two, I am happy to report, experienced great success in this world.

There are so many things to be wary of in this life. Moderation in all things—even speaking too much brings about ill-gotten gains. So, to put it simply, what is the secret to health?

"To dine well, and sleep well."

This is not my idea, but Grandma's. This is what Grandma once said in a television interview.

Chapter 5

Giving Back to Society

The GNP's Duty

"If you have money, there's nothing that can't be done." Or so they say. And this phrase has real-world implications in today's society. In societies such as this, there is no hope. How have we come to this?

We were not born just to earn money. Money is important, but there are more valuable things than money alone. Health, family, charity, scholarship, faith, etc. These are the ideas that we have to ponder.

In today's world, the family is broken, trust is broken, and the world is topsy-turvy…all because of this focus on money, money, money. That is why we must act against the zeitgeist of the times and create a world where, "There are some things that cannot be done with mere money." A meritocracy based on hard work and ability is the wish and duty I lay upon you grandchildren.

During the twentieth century, they say that society reached its Golden Age, but in these times, many innocents died, the environment became damaged very quickly, and over half of Earth's inhabitants are still living in dire conditions. This is due to materialism and having less of a focus on the mind. But when they open their eyes, they only talk of the economy.

The world's leaders also talk of "revitalizing the economy" and a "prosperous society," without thinking about "revitalizing ethics" or "creating a fair and equal society."

I'm not saying that the economy or an affluent society is not important. The problem is that if you think money is the be-all and the end-all, then you start believing that money can buy happiness.

After humans were created, humans created money. Money follows Man. So it follows that arising from human need, an economy and personal wealth were created.

The Republic of Korea says these days we are on the cusp of the personal income of one South Korean individual reaching about $30,000 USD. But the income, I say, must match the morality of the individual, which should also be valued at the same sum.

In the United Kingdom or Sweden of old, they have mastered the creation of the "welfare state," but what followed in its wake? For a while, the United Kingdom's economy crumbled, and Sweden experienced an uptick in suicides.

The problem of the welfare state is that when peoples' bellies are full and they are content in the nursing home, they tend to become lazier, and tend to work less or not at all. This goes against the principle of a human's basic need to work.

Do you know what saved Sweden even though it stayed a welfare state. It became a capitalist welfare state and is still a kingdom. "From the cradle to the grave" is what they called the system. Once born, the state would protect them and care for their citizens. Does this not seem ideal, like a Heaven on Earth?

Bread and circuses. Of course, they are important. But as I always say, a person's inherent needs take precedence before their moral lives. These needs refer to their need to eat, to be cured of illnesses, and even their funerals are arranged for by the state. The problem with this model is that people lose their zest for life and some of them commit suicide. Some have reasons for taking their own lives, but because their reasons remain, the state must keep abreast of these problems. Suicide remains a serious problem in Scandinavia.

This story is a little old, but while Grandpa was still very active in the workforce, I had lots of business dealings with Swedish people, so I know a little about their mindset.

"These people, they are going on a safari as part of their job training. Why do I have to deal with those who are lazy, and won't pay attention to work?"

This was one businessman's angry assessment. A man I know, I'm sorry to say.

A lazy man will never work because he's lazy, and an assiduous man will become jealous and not work, and if he's not lazy or hard-working, then he will fall into a pit of nothingness, and commit suicide...this is the problem with the current welfare state?

My dear grandchildren, why am I spending so long on this particular discourse? I want you all to gaze at society with unclouded eyes, and help in the creation of a moral state where morality is championed as highly as money.

Like it or not, we are bound together as a society and as a nation. Don't be a lemming, living as others did, and not thinking whilst watching the world go by. For those, who have no purpose for living, and they inevitably lose their humanity.

I dream of a warm society where we treat each other well. Are we on the right path? Are we moral? These are the questions you will face as you enter the workforce. This comprises what the ancient Chinese called "tiānxiàwéigōng," or the state exists for the common man and is owned by him.

My Generation's Failings

Only about sixty years ago, South Korea was one of the poorest countries in the world. Per person, the average income was about $67 USD, similar to the per capita income of poor countries such as Somalia back then. Your generation may not understand, but we were so poor we could not afford three meals a day. Starvation is one of the worst societal ills. It may be difficult to imagine but think of people who are starving for food. Starvation is a horrible plight. Taken to extremes, it can result in death.

That is why the first item on the agenda was to reduce the food shortage; we believed back then that resolving this issue would solve all our problems.

My generation, led by former South Korean president Park Jung-hee, focused on two things: food, or "bbang," which means bread in English, and the economy. We put all our efforts into bolstering the economy. Of course, we could only think of our economic plight, and our long-held traditions of morality were put on the back burner.

My generation, in about just thirty years, transformed the Republic of Korea from a struggling developing country into one of the "East Asian" tigers. It was the "miracle on the Han River." UNESCO hailed South Korea as the fastest country in the world to climb out of the developing nations' plight. President Park and his administration had done it: we had ushered in the twentieth century. To this day, I sincerely believe that without President Park, we wouldn't have made it this far.

But we lost something, as we roared full steam ahead. When we came to, we realized that our citizens' pockets were full, but our beautiful traditions were lost or hidden. Filial piety, etiquette, and the "seonbi mindset (Confucian scholar mindset)" are all cultural traditions worth admiring. We turned away from our traditions and our beautiful virtues and focused on the economy.

That is why our Korean society has run asunder, and immoral, all because of our focus on filling our bellies with our daily bread. There are lots to admire about my generation, but dear grandchildren, you must also realize our failures.

A focus on materialism prevents us from building an ideal society. Our cultural traditions that focus on one's mindset are the other wheel of a wagon. The economy must support the cultural rites of our ancestors in order for the wheel of fortune to turn.

A man does not live for bread alone, and by itself, it cannot buy happiness.

Why Do We Work?

The Ideal vs. Reality

We Koreans who live south of the 38th Parallel cannot view the beautiful Guryong Falls on Geumkang Mountain. Did you know that the tale of the woodcutter and the fairy originates from these falls?

Once upon a time lived a kind woodcutter who saved a deer from a hunter. The deer, thankful to the woodcutter for saving his life, whispers into his ear: "If you go to Gurong Falls, there are fairies that come down from Heaven and bathe in its waters. Hide the clothes of one of the fairies. She will be unable to return to Heaven and will have to marry you," he said.

The fairy that lost her clothes married the woodcutter and gave birth to two children. The deer had warned the woodcutter in advance that until she bore three children, he should not return her fairy clothing to her. But the woodcutter does not heed this warning, and returns the clothes to her upon the birth of the second child.

He was so happy that he had forgotten all about the deer's warning. The fairy, upon receiving her clothes again, abandons her husband and rises to the skies, with a child in each arm.

The woodcutter represents reality, and while he was far from her ideal, the fairy tried to love her husband and worked hard to be a good wife. But Heaven (the Ideal) beckoned, and it was not far from her mind, even with every passing hour.

And so it went that the fairy was able to reclaim her clothes. Her heart must have been full, for it was again filled with hope that she could reenter Heaven. But when she sees the eyes of her husband, the hope turns into despair. That she would have to part with her beloved husband tears her heart. So which shall she choose? The husband or Heaven? The fairy debates between the two. But the fairy, who had been wandering about anyway, ultimately leaves her husband for the skies.

From her behavior, I can see man's struggle between Reality and the Ideal. A desperate situation, however, presents itself, and the fairy chooses Heaven over her reality (her love for her husband).

She must have been sad to part with her husband, and the new unknown world that she was about to reenter would have scared her. However, she makes the more difficult choice. That man inches closer to Heaven is because of the likes of the fairy, who shows bravery in this instance.

There may have been fairies that would have stayed content with reality, birthing three babies and staying with their spouses. So are these fairies bad? No. They work hard, love hard, and stay loyal to their realities. This is important as well. Reality is that important.

Peter Drucker,• an economist, once said, "Most modern humans have a reliance on social systems as the foundation for their lives."

As soon as one is born, regardless of one's own intentions, a person becomes a member of a certain society. In this, there are no choices that can be made. Like it or not, a person must follow the laws of the country and the social practices of the country he was born to. When he enters the workforce, Reality will be different from his own Ideal, and cause strife. However, one cannot turn away from society or flatly refuse it; this is not wise. Walking the tightrope between the Reality and the Ideal is the best way to live.

In the case of the fairy, when one confronts Reality, one must do it head-on. But when the time comes, it does not mean that she must automatically return to Heaven when the opportunity presents itself. Both choices are correct; whether she stays with her husband (Reality) or whether she returns to Heaven (the Ideal).

As I have stated before, the Ideal and Reality blur and create society. Actions that nudge society along flow from this concept.

A real-life example of a person who confidently marries the Ideal and Reality is Kim Seong-su, a true pioneer who established *The Dong-A Ilbo* and Korea University. He is comparable to Rhee Syngman, a true Korean giant. Kim was loyal to Reality while incorporating the Ideal into it, and in doing so, became a paragon of modern Korean society.

During the Japanese occupation of Korea, he was an independence fighter and vowed to grow Korea's leaders. Kim created both the

• Peter F. Drucker (1909–2005) was an Austrian-American economist. He foresaw that the value of labor and capital would fall and knowledge would outpace them, in a future where intellectual capital would create a "knowledge economy." His works include: *The New Society* (1950), *The Age of Discontinuity* (1969) and *Managing in Turbulent Times* (1980).

aforementioned university and the newspaper.

The Japanese occupation of Korea started with the installment of the Japanese Governor-General of Korea, and his target was often newspapers and universities that would awaken Korean nationalism. The Japanese Governor-General of Korea was given absolute power, and he could shut down schools or newspapers at his will.

But *The Dong-A Ilbo*, with the erasure of the Japanese flag,• awakened the independence movement of Korea, and a high school that had been created along with Korea University enrolled every student who had been expelled due to partaking in the independence movement.

They angered the Japanese Governor-General of Korea. They also opposed the colonial policy found in books. It is a miracle that the newspaper and the university have survived to date. With Kim's brilliance at reconciliation and stoking the independence spirit, he single-handedly, at every turn, prevented the closure of the school and the shutting down of the newspaper.

I have heard that some nowadays point to Kim having been a Japanese collaborator, and they even took back the Order of Merit for founding the country from him. How absurd is the world we are living in today?

He was the one who poured his own personal fortune into establishing the high school, university, and newspaper; all these were distasteful for the Japanese back then. Kim was larger-than-life, with larger-than-life plans. So what if he did win arguments with his

• In August 1936, two newspapers, *The Dong-A Ilbo* and *The Chosun JoongAng Ilbo*, printed the winner of the marathon from the Berlin Olympics, Sohn Kee-Chung, without the Japanese flag. T*he Chosun JoongAng Ilbo* was shut down. *The Dong-A Ilbo* ceased publication from August 27th, but was revived nine months later.

brilliance over why the schools and the newspaper shouldn't be shut down? He used his brilliant oratory powers to save the schools and the newspaper.

It's horrifying to think that *The Dong-A Ilbo* and Korea University may have closed without the help of Kim during the Japanese occupation of Korea. For many times, they were in danger of being shut down by the Japanese Governor-General himself. It would have been our loss.

Not every man can reform and lead in the development of society. Dreams (the Ideal) are usually individualistic, and not pluralistic. If you lead with a warped view of an Ideal, then reformations will lead to people being in worse straits than before.

For far too long, communism has made our society despair, and we must learn from this tragedy. It's a harsh lesson for us to learn.

Occupation

"What kind of work can I do once I enter the workplace?" This is a good question.

When you select your job, the first thing you should consider is your true nature, and the second is your dreams. The first should come first. That is the way to live fully in the present reality and is the shortcut to doing well.

Your dreams are tomorrow's problems, while reality is today's problem. You must tackle today's problem first. You have to succeed today, in order to achieve your dreams tomorrow.

When you think of earning money, you should not think of how you are going to spend it (dreams) first. How can you achieve your dreams when you are incapable of earning money?

The stupid ones are the ones with money and no dreams. If those who have earned a lot of money spend it badly, then it will only hurt society. Money that you put in the bank is better than the money you have spent on drink, and if you send money to an orphanage, so much the better; the money becomes even more valuable.

While you should select your occupation with what fits your abilities and personality, if you can somehow tie that in with your dreams, then the job will be your best fit. When you are selecting your job, if possible, select one that will be of service to many.

"The one who makes the arrow worries that the arrow won't pierce the armor, while the one who makes the armor worries that the person who is wearing it may become hurt," according to Mencius. In this instance, isn't it better to select the job of being the armorer?

But dear grandchildren, "Why should we work?" Work is like raising crops, making a plow, earning money…you get something, and you do something for others. This means you make something and do something to achieve something, but the most important part is the sweat you put into it. This is the "working spirit."

During the Lu Dynasty in the Spring and Autumn Period once lived a man who asked his mother, "Mother, I am a government official, and yet, why do you weave for a living?" He tried to get his mother to stop working.

Then his mother said, "The Lu Dynasty will fall if everyone acted like you. That they put a thoughtless boy in the position of a government official…Sit. If you think of the people working, then this will make you feel kinder towards others. If the people do not work, they will turn lustful, then will lose the good. That the people are well-behaved on dry land in need of water is because they work."

That is why the first order of business is to "work."

The second is to benefit others. "To plant and harvest crops." This is to feed others. It's not just for feeding oneself and one's family. "To teach," means to grow another person's heart and mind. "To play the piano" is to give others joy. Big or small, all these things are for the benefit of others.

The third that you reap is self-realization.

As I have mentioned in the previous pages, it is also good to realize your dreams. Set a goal, and work towards the goal with all your might; through this process comes self-realization, or knowing how to live as you will.

The fourth is the sweet taste of success. There are times when you will be successful. There are times when you will fail. When you do well, you will feel splendid. When you don't do as well, you will feel awful. This is the nature of work; sometimes you will succeed, and sometimes you won't. Failure hurts, but success…your heart will swell with joy. Self-realization comes about as the evolution of your dreams complete and is closely tied with inspiration. That you managed to pull off something that others did not, or could not do, is like climbing to the top of the mountain and savoring sweet success. If these did not pay off, then why do we ski or play tennis? Wouldn't it be like manual labor?

The fifth is to earn money. You earn money, honor, and prestige. A person is by nature, selfish. Without selfishness, mankind would not have made it this far. The problem lies in selfishness that knows no bounds and tramples over others as a despotic monster. Only self-control will appease this trait in man, and lend itself to creation and inspiration. This will be the seed of self-discipline.

Go to Work Thirty Minutes Early

When you finish your schooling, it's off to work for you. In the workplace, you must work for the good of others, work for self-realization, and find meaning. But society is not all golden. Of course, it will be different from school. Your companions have also gone through school. But at that stage of life, they did not try to trip you up. If you did extremely well in your studies, then they couldn't touch you.

In the workplace, someone is trying to trip you, at every stage. If you are doing better than someone, then they will shoot you from behind. You think your enemies are the only ones who do this? It could be your best friend. Alas, you think this is bad? Sometimes even your superiors stomp on you. This is the current state of the workplace in today's very human society. It's all good and well, finding the meaning and achieving self-realization, but remember, first and foremost, stay alive. That is why talent is necessary.

"Our well rope is short, and just look, the neighbors' well is very deep." "The grass is always greener on the other side," is a similar adage in English. This aforementioned phrase is found in *Myungshimbogam (Míngxīnbǎojiàn)*.•

Your life's success cannot be measured at the tennis court. Or the size of your house. You will sweat at work, and not the tennis court, otherwise, you will not survive. The winner will be decided in the workplace. Heed my warning.

You may dream of a sugar-spun future, where "I will earn money to

• This book dates back to the Goryeo Dynasty of Korea, with the primary goal of instructing persecuted children on how to treat others (benignly, of course). During the Joseon Dynasty, the book was widely used as a primer at local schools.

buy a house, then rise up the ranks until I become CEO." If only it were that easy.

If the workplace were full of fools, then the world would be easy. But the worst part of it is that the real nasty fools don't know what competition is and yet mess up by being jealous of your success. If they are good competitors, then at least you can bring up the subject of fair play. But they are full of rudeness. That is why society is difficult, and robs you of your breath, and is noisy.

You need real talent and need real sweat at the workplace. It's difficult to run, and yet, a real race will test your mettle. If you complain that the rope is too short, then you will always lose. Fault the deep well, and you will only receive censure.

"Then what can I do?" This is something that Hyo Jung used to say when she was not even two years old. When I think back upon it, she used to say this habitually.

So how can you survive in such harsh conditions in the workplace? Do not be afraid. No matter how cruel the conditions and the competition may be, there will always be a silver lining behind every cloud. And if there isn't, so what? Recognize those who exceed you in talent silently. Your opponent will not be a ghost. I'm human after all, and wouldn't mind a good, fair fight.

The solution is simple. "When you jump once, I jump twice. If you work for a day, I work for two days." Promise this to yourself. "I will work twice that of others," is the resolve you must make.

If you want to win in a competition, then you must have innate talent, but this accounts for maybe 10 percent of the total population. About 90 percent, I believe, is based on hard work. If you are determined to lose, then so be it, but if you are aiming to win, then you must work twice as hard. If you are jumping and I am jumping, then are you going to say that jumping once will be enough to place you first? From the onset, you'll start off on the wrong foot.

"Those who sow in tears will reap with songs of joy," Psalms 126:5. God will see your sweat and tears, and bring you the sweet joy of success.

Let's move on.

Let us say that you will arrive at work thirty minutes before others. This is the first step. This is also what I told your father, Hyo Jung, when he started his first job. You know how it is; during rush hour, five minutes is precious. If you take thirty golden minutes to arrive before the morning hustle, it will pay off tremendously. It's better to be an hour early, even.

If you avoid the morning rush hour, you won't get stuck in traffic. There will be only a few people at the office, and no calls made so early, either. If you start work thirty minutes before others, then your productivity will increase and you can finish the work that you've failed to do in time. You will be named as an assiduous employee by your boss and earn his trust, etc.

The next is a social currency in the workplace. If you are ostracized, then you will not survive. That is why even if you are exceptionally talented, you must not incur the wrath or jealousy of others. This is why your eccentric behavior may buy you the awe of others, but looked at in a different light, you may be a freak, and selfish as they come. No wonder why they look at you oddly. The solution to this is social currency.

In human relationships, the real key is modesty. There are many foolish people who boast. This is like spending money and earning others' censure. You are creating small holes that will make the lifeboat sink.

As you age, you will realize that social ties can be broken by the silliest of things, and not events great or small.

Some examples include: "That person doesn't say hello," "She has no filter when she speaks," and or, "She's pretending." Please take heed to greet others, and give way to others' will, then nothing will be out of the ordinary. Pride goes before a fall. Many people, because they are too proud, upend an important assignment because of these fallacies that I mention here.

During the Song Dynasty, a man named "Hyo Woo" once said, "Even if you give right of way to another, there will be no instance of bowing a hundred times to him, and even if you give your plot of land to another, you will not sink to a lower level."

The *Talmud* says, "The greatest wisdom of all is modesty." Even Lao Tzu said, "Modesty speaks to the Heavens." They were not exaggerating.

The next are kindred spirits. It's difficult to achieve anything on one's own. Once you enter society, you must have allies. In the workplace, there will be at least one or two who will want to befriend you. It can be a superior or a subordinate. You must pick a good person. But it's difficult to pick a good person. Even I fail at this sometimes. I have trusted the wrong men too many times, so shall we listen to a sage first?

"There are three good friends and three bad ones. The honest man will be the friend, and the trustworthy friend will be the friend, and the scholarly man will be the last friend. If you take the person who is ill-mannered as a friend, or a flatterer as a friend, or a person who doesn't keep his promises as a friend, then you welcome in suffering."

"The one who points out my mistakes is my teacher, the one who treats me as an in-law is my friend, and the one who flatters me is my enemy."

All can be found in Hsun-tzu's writings about cultivating one's morals.

This is a bit difficult, isn't it?

Then let's think for a moment. You must be a modest person, at first. But you must not grovel. A really strong person is modest, while a weak one sometimes appears modest. You should heed my warning against the second's bluff.

The next goal is to be a healthy person. If you are more brawny than anything else, then it is not good, and you must be realistic. You must not prevaricate, but be honest. A man who is puffed up with pride is not to my liking either—if you follow these guidelines, my goodness, it seems that picking the right friends is even more difficult than finding a spouse. If you are too picky, then I fear that marriage may pass you by in this life.

Grandpa chooses the "silent one" first to befriend. The less he talks, the more likely he may be untalented and stupid, but the majority of them are sincere.

The *Talmud* says, "The donkey can be recognized by its long ears, and the foolish man can be recognized by his long tongue." My experience tells me that talkative men are dispensable.

Maybe things are different between women. A depressed person is not a beautiful person to befriend. Instead of such a person, why not take the cheerful talkative one as a friend? I'll stop here.

When you finally mature in thought and mind, you will find that there are few people in this world who are faultless. "An angel's best trait is that he has no faults, and man's best trait is that he does." We can even go so far as to say, "The person is honest because he did not have an opportunity to steal." These phrases are from the *Talmud*. Man will always have faults, and make mistakes.

When you are evaluating a person or choosing a person, you must look for qualities to praise rather than censure.

You are not searching for a marriage partner. You are searching for a kindred spirit. The very word, "dongji," in Korean, means "together, with one goal in mind." You can choose someone who may have some faults, but at least one strength. These kindred spirits will stay with you in the harsh world of today.

Grandpa had a terrible year. This terrible annus horribilis was in 1987. On the outside, I was calm, but inside, I was shuddering with rage and despair. Every day was a challenge.

And then thanks to serendipity, my American friend, Glenn, came to me. "Rocky, you are my friend. I can be your enemy or your friend. You choose. Either way, even if the whole world turns its back on you, I will be your friend forever." My heart ached from joy. He called me Rocky, and I call him Glenn.

A friend you do not make easily. You have to cultivate friendship, like a person tends to a beautiful garden. You will have to put in lots of effort, much more so, in order to gain a true friend. A true friend is a beautiful thing.

Confucius says, "A true compliment is worth more than a thousand bars of gold."

How to achieve this is outlined thus: through small, random acts of kindness.

Compliments can be a good thing. Don't be afraid to use them. "Good job on today's lecture," you can say, while drinking coffee with them, and "this seminar's topic and content was really good." These are just examples.

Be grateful for every act of kindness, however small…

"Hey, thanks for the musical tickets. I really enjoyed myself. I haven't been to the theater in two years."

The point is, "jeongseong (sincere heart)," works every single time. Fake sincerity and you will inevitably sink.

Spend time together. Dine with them, go fishing, and hiking, but remember, no money should exchange hands. You will lose money and lose your friend. If you have the means, then just give them a monetary gift. That is preferable to loaning money.

In order to reach peoples' hearts, you must be sincere. It's not a fake affect. The art of living does not apply to winning friendships. They are acquaintances, not friends.

In the *Sohak*, there are some sayings worth noting: "You will not lose the country if the feudal lords are served by kind knights. A gentleman of good breeding who has three true friends will never lose his dignity and his good family standing will remain intact. For the *seonbi* (Confucian scholar), if he has a servant who points out his errors, then he should remain forever grateful."

"To us Americans, we have a best friend. We stand facing each other and watch each others' backs." So said Glenn many years ago.

Who Will Wear the Laurel Wreath?

Conviction and Bravery

Who puts the laurel wreath on the winner after a marathon? It is the chairman of the competition. Because he won.

Who will promote you at work? It is the CEO. Because you have been effective at your work.

Success comes from doing well yourself; it does not involve others' work.

In the *Talmud*, it says, "Do not fault the rat, but the rat hole." Do not fault the chairman of the competition for not crowning you with the laurel wreath; fault yourself instead. When you fail in the real world, it is because you have not closed the "rat holes." Do not fault the rat. If you want the laurel wreath, you have to win. Don't focus on the chairman's face to gauge his moods.

In order to win, you must put in your best efforts and fight, fight, fight. Even this may be insufficient. You have to have a strategy, be resourceful, and have patience.

The laurel wreath represents success, and it does not come for free.

What is the secret to success? It is bravery and conviction.

Be bold. Be daring. Throw everything you have at them and knock them dead!

Some people preach prudence and caution. But this is only while sitting, in my point of view. Once you hit the ground running, you have to leave caution behind.

A Korean saying says, "You have to knock even a stone bridge before crossing it." Should you knock it? It's OK to knock it, but nearly all people do not cross the stone bridge even after knocking it. That is why the bold person wins.

The more important it is, the more serious it is, I preach boldness instead of caution. This is paramount to success. You will realize this later.

Caution is a very scary thing. Do not think of failure at any turn. Always believe that it can be done and that you can win. Thoughts become actions, and beliefs become a realization of a dream long held dear.

If you have no confidence in doing a task well, pray. Pray fervently.

Belief gives you confidence, and this confidence will give you the laurel wreath that you seek.

Do you not already know of the subconscious? Read "The Magic of Conviction" one more time. If you feel that this is inadequate, then read some verses from the Good Book.

"Therefore I tell you, whatever you ask for in prayer, believe that you have received it, and it will be yours" (Mark 11:24).

Ignore Slander

As you live, do not be afraid of slander and betrayal. Nothing hurts more, and makes us despair, but do not lose your nerve. It's always the sketchy character that commences with the cursing.

Our family is honest, and therefore, dignified.

Even Jesus Christ was betrayed by an average man. Do not despair before betrayal and fall to your knees because of slander, for nothing in the world can be achieved if you fall victim to others' (ill-advised) censure.

"The spring rain is like oil to the person who is traveling, and the thief dislikes the bright autumn moon for its brightness." This can be found in the *Myungshimbogam.*

The world is full of logic such as this, so how can you expect to hear only good reports and praise?

When you are betrayed, think of Judas. Judas sold Jesus Christ for a pittance by today's standards, and Peter the Apostle ran away and swore he did not know Jesus three times in a single day.

When you hear censure, close your ears and your lips. Silence is the best weapon. There is no need to respond. That would be the worst type of response. But keep your eyes steady. Do not gaze disapprovingly or laugh ironically.

Once, a man tripped an old man. The old man stood up and smiled wide. The other man was struck speechless. What if he had thought of fighting back? Then who would have been in the right? To ignore requires patience and courage, and this is one such example.

In 1987, a daily newspaper libeled me. My friends pressed me to press charges. But I merely pursed my lips and refused to speak.

"When they beat you up and you show no response, then the other party will lose their strength." This is what one prominent journalist said to me at the time.

The former U.S. President Abraham Lincoln is a man who was both greatly revered and yet, denounced. He once admitted that if he had responded to every bitter diatribe thrown at him, then he would not have been able to lead the nation during the American Civil War before his death.

"I will follow my beliefs, no matter what anyone says. To me, diatribes are not important, but success in my work is what I hold dear. If the work's outcome suffers, then even if a thousand angels sing their praises to me, it matters not," he said.

He framed these words and hung them on a wall in his office, and General MacArthur, during the Korean War, hung this phrase at the desk headquarters.

Some do give well-deserved censure. But most of them who say such things are not good people and are lacking in at least the social graces. That is why I would like to use the word slander instead, and that means that most of the censure that you receive will be undeserved.

Slander will accompany you as you go about your work, and if you fall into a very bad situation, you will see people who put others down like clockwork. But such is life! I am afraid you may be disappointed. Read this and be kind to yourself.

During the Great Flood, all sorts of animals came to Noah's ark. A good man ran to Noah and asked for safety from the Flood. Noah said unto him, that he could not admit him, because he had no partner. The good man ran into the forest and came back with Evil.

This is a story from the *Talmud.*

This is paramount to the duality of nature and the universe. Good and Evil, Night and Day, Female and Male, the Sun and the Moon—everything in this world exists like Yin and Yang. These opposites make a whole.

In Eastern philosophy, we call this "yin." Buddhism says that polar opposites are actually one, and two halves of a whole. In modern Physics, we call this "Sangboseong (Mutual Supplementation)."

Is it possible to ignore slander directed against oneself and slander others' instead? The worst thing to do is throw barbs at someone else. This is slander, this is judgment.

For our family, let us keep this promise.

"Never slander others."

There are some who take out their frustrations on a server at a restaurant.

"I ordered ginseng tea, not coffee! You drink it!"

For you, this might be the first time the server has made a mistake, but for him, he has been harassed by customers all day. He's cantankerous and his blood starts to boil. His feet hurt him.

"You brought coffee. I ordered ginseng tea! Well, if you were busy, I'm sure you must've just gotten confused."

Isn't this beautiful?

"Judge not, that ye be not judged" (Matthew 7:1).

Failure Is a Teacher

Do not fear failure. Failure is a teacher. It's a teaching in disguise.

"In order to prognosticate the future, read the signs." Success makes us tempt Fate and makes fools of us all.

Success is a friend, while failure is a teacher. If you only like your friend and do not pay attention to your teacher, then how will you learn?

Let's talk baseball. Babe Ruth hit 714 home runs during his lifetime. This was a world record at the time. But he struck out 1,330 times. But people remember his accomplishments and not his failures.

The Jewish are a wise people.

Mistakes

Everyone has a flaw or two, and a person is bound to make a mistake sometimes. Sometimes he sins without knowing.

But in the *Talmud*, a person who has a perfect record of shooting arrows sometimes is unable to adjust to an ever-changing clime. Everyone tries his best to live an honest and assiduous life, and yet, humans are fallible.

In the *Talmud*, it also says, "When a man marries, he sins a lot." This is the sticking point, the nail in the coffin.

When you have made a mistake, what should you do? Pray and repent. Sincerely regret the mistake. This is what constitutes Man.

The *Talmud* says, "The place where one who repents the most is holier than the place where a distinguished rabbi lives."

Even God forgives he who repents.

Moral Conviction and Keeping the Body in Line with the Faith

Before commencing, I would like to refer to the Eastern philosophical teachings of the sages.

"A person who keeps himself clean must only follow these three commandments: integrity, prudence, and diligence." This is found in the *Tóngměngxùn* or a textbook I referred to before meant for children in the East.

"Be wary of celebrating others' bad faults or deeds. That in itself is shameful. Instead, celebrate your neighbor's kind deeds, and help others. You may be able to save them in a time of need," Confucius says.

Zengzi says, "Confucius said that there are three ways that must all be followed to live properly as Man. The first is to move one's own body in a mannerly fashion, which will make violence depart. The second is to change one's complexion by lighting it with goodness. Then you will buy the other's trust. Finally, the third is to keep your language polite and on point, then you will leave forcefulness and meanness behind."

In the *Talmud*, it says, "A real wise man will act thusly. When he meets someone, he will always think of the other as superior to him in a certain area. If he is older than you, then revere him because he must be an excellent person. He must have had more opportunities to shine because he had more opportunities to do good work. When he is younger than you, then think that he must have sinned less than you. If he lives a more lavish existence than you, then believe that he must have done more charitable works, and marvel at him. If he is poorer than you, then he must have withstood more pain while living, and regard him with sympathy. If he is wiser than you, then heed his wisdom. If he is less wise than you, then you will choose to believe that the cup is half full and that he has sinned less than you."

This is also from the *Talmud*.

"To be a sensible person, follow these guidelines. Firstly, in front of someone who is wiser than you, stay silent. Secondly, do not interrupt another's conversation. Thirdly, do not respond and explain too quickly. Fourthly, ask the questions that get to the heart of the matter. Fifthly, do what needs to be done first, then do the rest that can be postponed for later. Sixthly, acknowledge it if you do not know. Seventhly, recognize truth and acknowledge it."

I am quoting from the classics because I have yet to be as wise.

One of the hardest things I had to do as an individual was to differentiate between public and private lives. Whenever someone enters the workforce, they should heed "seongonghusa," or make a clear distinction between public and private. Many people make mistakes at work not because they lack talent, but because they put their personal interests above that of the company.

Dear grandchildren, when you get a job in the real world, remember "seongonghusa," and abide by it. If you put personal interests before the interests of the company, then you are not ready to enter the workforce.

The Art of Manners

In order to succeed in the workplace, you must have manners and speak well. Today's society dictates a "global" workplace so there are some Western manners that you should be aware of.

In the fourteenth century, a man named William of Wykeham established the New College at the University of Oxford. Its slogan, to this day, remains, "Manners makyth man."

The history of the British gentleman stretches back far in time. In society, manners, and how one conducts oneself, matter just as much as knowledge, a hundred times over.

In the East, there is an ancient book of etiquette I would like to refer to: "Do not lean on the wall and eavesdrop. When answering, do not answer in a high and hurried voice. Do not cursorily gaze at another, and do not be slow and lazy in your movements, and at the same time, do not slack off. When you walk, you must not swagger, and when you stand, do not lean on one leg, and when you sit, do not stretch your legs out, and when you sleep, do not sleep on your belly. Your hair should be carefully braided and not unkempt, and you should keep your 'gat'(a kind of hat with a wide brim that traditional Korean gentleman wears) on, and do not roll up your sleeves because you are tired and do not roll up your pants legs because it is hot."

Manners maketh man, and even in the East, this holds true.

In the West, people, upon first meeting, make the following observations.

Firstly, when they shake hands, is their grip firm?

Secondly, where do their eyes go during the course of the conversation?

Thirdly, is their posture good?

In the East, handshakes are not the custom, but remember, it takes one hand and a firm grip. Also, while in the East it is traditionally frowned upon to gaze directly at another, nowadays, we must look directly at the other person as well.

Another type of etiquette worth knowing is table manners. They say in the West when hiring someone or promoting someone, they invite them to dine and observe their table manners. If they do not know how to handle their silverware, for example, remember that they may not get hired or promoted.

You must read books on Western etiquette.

There is another aspect of manners that must be discussed.

It has to do with one's attire. As they say in the East, your clothes give you wings, so when you enter the real world, you must pay attention to your appearance.

In the West, they say, "In your village, you are evaluated by your reputation, but elsewhere, you are judged by your clothing."

In Shakespeare's *Hamlet*, isn't there a section where Polonius, the chief counselor to the king, tells his son, Laertes, to pay attention to his clothing and all manners of his attire?

It's to do with cleanliness, not so much the price.

In attire, there are also trends. It has to fit the place and the circumstances. It must also make you look regal. Therefore, color and design are paramount to life itself. At least make yourself listen to the wise counsel of an expert. I recommend the Color Me Mine's test.

Manners may maketh man, but your manner of speaking also makes you uniquely yourself. How well you speak is now determined by speaking eloquently and volubly.

Do not be confused by sweet talk. This is actually off-limits. What does it mean to speak restrainedly? It means to speak less. Only say that which is necessary. "Talk with your eyes" instead. This is an excellent teaching from the East.

In the West, there is an emphasis on manners, and in the East, we stress the need to talk to less, very much so. Without a doubt, there are many Eastern sages who have much to say about the value of speaking with restraint.

According to Confucius, "A person of yesteryear does not speak without thinking, because actions matter more than words, and he is afraid that the action may not rise to the occasion." He also teaches him to be assiduous and thoughtful while speaking.

In the *Book of Odes*, it warns, "A white marble that has a mark on it becomes useless because you cannot smooth away the mark, and the smear left by my words cannot be taken away."

Silence is a virtue, and in the East, there are so many wise words of merit that render me speechless to this day.

On Praise

The best part of the art of conservation lies in praise. Praise is one of the best virtues. "Praises can even make a whale dance," according to a Western adage that I am paraphrasing here. Praise can dictate destiny, and determine the fate of a nation, as I am sure countless examples can attest.

Praise is one of the arts in conversation that has the power to make friends, make amends, and even erase immense debt. Does it not have the power of miracles?

During World War I, Germany was defeated and the Emperor Wilhelm II earned the censure of all, or so it may have seemed. Even from his countrymen, he was so unpopular that he was in danger of being assassinated.

A young German boy wrote him a letter, saying, which I will paraphrase here, "No matter what anyone says, I will always regard you, dear Emperor, as my King." The Kaiser Wilhelm II was deeply moved and in a heartfelt reply, expressed his wish to meet the boy.

The young boy, accompanied by his mother, went to visit the

Emperor. Some time passed, and the mother of the boy ended up marrying the Emperor. This is a real story. The boy's praise had brought this miracle about.

In nineteenth-century Great Britain, former Prime Minister, Benjamin Disraeli and William E. Gladstone• were two formidable politicians known to many around the world. They were the men of the day and had many political rivals. As such, they left many anecdotes worth noting.

But in my view, Disraeli sets the benchmark, and a passage from a book I have recently read confirms this view.

"I invited both men to dine with me two evenings in a row, one after the other. When I bid Gladstone goodbye, I realized that in Great Britain, he was the wisest. While bidding Disraeli goodbye, I realized that I was the wisest female in Great Britain."

With almost certainty, I am sure that Gladstone was full of his opinions and philosophies, while Disraeli kept on praising the woman who had invited him to dine with her.

Rather than praising your life philosophy and skills, it is better to praise the other; this is of a higher nature, and a sophisticated way of living, or savoir vivre.

Twice, Queen Victoria•• appointed Disraeli prime minister, and everyone knows this as a fact, but there must have been a way he managed to secure this post. As he confessed later, he curried favor with the Queen via praise.

• William E. Gladstone (1809–1898) was a famous British politician who served as Prime Minister for four terms. Along with Benjamin Disraeli, he shaped parliamentary politics in Great Britain during the nineteenth century.

•• Queen Victoria (1819–1901) was regent for sixty-four years, and while ruling Great Britain, saw its empire rise to dizzying heights ("the Empire where the sun never sets").

As an aside, Disraeli was never known to have protested in his own favor…ever.

There are many books on the power of praise, and I pray you will read them at least once. Andrew Carnegie• once said that, "The power that praise could wield could transform one into a millionaire or a great politician."

The *Talmud* also says, "When someone asks for your opinion on a building one has already bought, even if the building is not to your liking, say 'it is a fine building.' If a friend has already married, even if you have to lie, say 'your wife is a great beauty.'"

I would hesitate to say compliments are lies. This is a piece of Jewish wisdom.

Humor

In the art of talking, there is another that is almost as important, and this is humor. Humor comes before the art of conversing, and it gives life its sheen, and is instrumental in maintaining one's health.

Humor gives liveliness to a conversation, and can shake the feelings and even the souls of those who are conversing together. Even more, the people around them and cast a spell of enchantment on all of them.

They say that the British have an excellent sense of humor, but the reason this is so is because in Great Britain, they regard humor as the highest form of refinement.

Humor is elegant, and there is a tendency to exclude those without it in conversation.

The reason why the United Kingdom was able to withstand World

• Andrew Carnegie (1835–1919) was a Scottish-born American industrialist who was named the "Steel King." In his later years, he established foundations for public works.

War II was in part due to humor.

During the Blitzkrieg, people shuddered with fear in the Underground. But there is an urban legend saying that someone with a sense of humor rallied those around him by making them laugh. Does it not seem that then humor is a virtue, and an elegant one at that?

Humor, as I said before, has the ability to raise the bar in conversation. It also has the ability to breathe life into dull moments. It is one of the ways to live life leisurely.

Do Not Damage the Other Person with Words

There is a danger between friends conversing, and that is this: do not go beyond debating, that is, do not argue and humiliate your friend.

A debate where you win over your opponent with excellent reasoning skills does not force him to submit to you. Your sense of self-worth may be elevated, but how would the other person feel? He may be angry and humiliated and perhaps even harbor resentment. In other words, you may just lose a friend. Words are a tool to win, not a tool to humiliate.

In the *Sohak*, there is a saying, "You must express your point of view in an honest way, and you must not insist on your point of view getting across to the other person."

Our ancestors are truly remarkable and wise.

Manners Are a Type of Vigor

I fear that I am talking too much about the art of conversation, but as such, it is such an important topic that I wish to do justice to it.

But according to some books on conversing eloquently, the best technique actually lies in listening well.

According to the *Talmud*, it says, "The reason why we have two ears and one mouth is for us to listen twice that of speaking."

Manners and the art of talking eloquently are both good ways to bolster your circle of friends and acquaintances. I warned against too much eloquence, and manners must not end in just skillfully executing them.

In manners, elegance and grace are important. When I refer to a person's aura, it refers to the whole person, sometimes warm, sometimes dry, sometimes irresistibly determined, saying a thousand words with just one look. Likewise, if on a spring day there is a brook with melted snow, there is a high mountain and depth to the waters, and while your two feet are on the ground your mind soars high above.

How do you grow your aura into that of a dignified one?

A Confucian scholar and politician during the Joseon Dynasty named Yulgok Yi I may have some answers. First, make your steps heavy. Second, gather your hands modestly. Third, gaze straight ahead. Fourth, close your mouth. Fifth, modulate your voice. Sixth, hold your head straight and high. Seventh, modulate your breathing, eighth, stand straight, ninth, make your complexion comfortable.

This is found in the third chapter of his book *Introduction to Ways of Life*.

You must train your mind and body. Manners speak to your vigor as a human being.

Become Better at Work

Making Good Use of Time

Some people are just good at their jobs. They refer to these people having ability, but there are few who are truly exceptional. Mozarts and

Einsteins, for example, how many do you think exist in this world?

Our society consists of average men congregating and doing business. Whether one does one's job well depends not on ability but assiduousness and a sense of responsibility. If I were to add to this formula, then I would add how he makes use of his time.

Responsibility and assiduousness are both prerequisites, so I am going to speak more at length about using one's time wisely.

When you think upon it, there is something magical about Time. It is decisive and has a wide-ranging effect on Man.

Man is born, then dies, as do all living things on this Earth. Indeed, the whole universe was created by the Big Bang and will die according to Time.

Then what is Time? I don't know. When the Big Bang occurred, Time and Space expanded at a rapid pace, but how far it will go (it is actually accelerating) I do not know and I fear mankind does not know. Only God may know.

Grandpa thinks that the success and failure of the world's comings and goings and doings are due to Time.

A certain rabbi once said, "Time is not money, but life." Then he asked, "How much time do you have left in your Timebank?"

This is a scary question. He implies that one has to use Time effectively and wisely.

You cannot bank Time, nor borrow Time, and thus you cannot compare it to money.

Time is fair. You cannot keep it bound. As I said before, Time waits for no Man.

I think, as the Good Book says, there is a time for everything. If you miss the timing, you will mess up in work. Additionally, as you have been lazy, you have wasted Time. If you have competitors, you are already twice behind.

Then how to manage Time effectively?

The first is to make a plan. How will you make use of Time? You must make a plan and a goal. If you are too greedy about achieving the goal too quickly, you may despair in the middle, and if you run out of time, you will never finish. In more complex terms, this is what is called, the "Doctrine of the Mean," or "moderation." You need not worry. If you read the whole book, you will understand.

You must set a goal, but I always set at least two; one in the middle, and one for the end. That is how you stay motivated and at the midpoint, you can change some variables to better fit your end goal.

So I made plans. Plans for the day, and plans for the future, some stretching as far as ten years, and even further. This may scare you because it is grandiose. Afterwards, you should read an economics text.

With regard to my ten-year plan, I am going to give you an example from my personal life.

In 1986, the Republic of Korea was about to open the 10th Asian Games. In 1985, the South Korean government made plans ahead of this international event and stressed innovation. Each sport's organization (and execution, including funding) would be headed by a South Korean conglomerate CEO.

With only a year left to go, it was essential to bring in business leaders making the event more effective.

I, as the KEPCO head, was given the track and field division. Other large companies (conglomerates) also were assigned a sport or division, and Samsung was assigned wrestling, Hyundai got swimming, POSCO got gymnastics, LG got canoeing, and Hanhwa was assigned boxing. And so on and so forth.

This was my first time being in charge of a sporting event, but I had confidence, because I had already been in charge of running a business at a large corporation. The rules of engagement for running a company and running a sporting event are one and the same.

As I said before, I made plans delineated by time. In order to make good plans, you need to know the personality of the task at hand, so I analyzed and picked a strategy. I selected the targets and made an end goal.

We only had one year and six months until the Asian Games. I couldn't select too many targets. In an Olympiad, in the sector of track and field, there are over forty medals to be awarded, the most of any sporting event.

In my targets, I decided to focus on ten of them. These included the 100m and the 200m dash, the mid-distance 800m, the long-distance 5000m, and the marathon in the track division, and in the field division, the long jump and the high jump.

In each target area, I made short-term plan and mid-to-long-range plans and set goals for each of them. In the midst of all this, I decided to forgo the marathon, as we only had one year and six months… too short a time period to reach the benchmark already set by world medalists.

But in truth, I set a ten-year plan for the marathon. While it wouldn't be a target of the 1986 Asian Games, I called it "The ten-year reconstruction plan for the marathon."

If I may be so bold, I will let the results speak for themselves. In the Asian Games, South Korea won a bronze. Seven years later, at the Barcelona Olympiad, Hwang Young-cho won a gold medal. And at the following Olympics held in Atlanta, Georgia, USA, Lee Bong-ju won a silver. The two of them raised the status of the marathon for South

Korean sports.

So how did the 1986 Asian Games go?

At the beginning, I believed that in the division of track and field, we would at the most win two golds. But we ended up winning seven.

This was thanks to everyone setting good plans in advance.

I would like to mention here an old sage who planned his life not just with a ten-year plan, but in entirety.

In China, during the Song Dynasty, lived a man named Zhū xīnzhòng. He was thinking of five plans that would define his life.

The first plan was living. What would he do to earn a living and pay for his bread and board?

The second plan was plans for good health. In other words, how would he live a healthy life?

The third plan was for family. As the head, how would he teach his family and his descendants?

The fourth was for old age. How would he spend his days as a retiree?

The fifth was for dying. We live but once. How would he prepare for death?

Is this not an excellent teaching? It's over eight hundred years old. I have seen it replicated in the current field of modern Economics.

In Economics, there are many detailed plans regarding the establishment of plans. Short and mid-to-long-term plans and the importance of setting goals, and hitting each goal in the mid-to-long term, are some of the important methods that are being taught today.

Do Not Procrastinate

What Grandpa wishes to stress is to read the signs and the Time.

Especially in terms of when to start. If you miss the timing, then you will miss the ability to succeed. Failure starts in most instances because we miss the timing.

But to read the signs and get the timing right is really difficult. Even Confucius, as wise as he was, admitted that he wasn't confident about his timing.

Confucius says that there is a time for everything, and called this, "shizhong." Isn't this difficult? It's OK to not know it. Grandpa doesn't know it either.

So why do we do this? When you are of age, you may understand what Grandpa meant to convey here.

If I do attempt to explain it here, it is that there are too many things in this world that are unknowable. That is how difficult this world is. But know this: the world is difficult. That is why we have to be modest. But a humble heart that prays and asks wholeheartedly is able to know a little bit more.

I will now teach you a method that I have used before.

Knowing "shizhong" is very difficult. But in order to be as close as possible to "shizhong," you must not procrastinate. This is also known as "sokjeonsokkyeol," or "An intensive swift attack," or in other words, handle a matter with more haste than with caution.

There is another saying, called "jolsok." This happens when you hasten a task. This is not a good saying.

The antonym to this is "sinjung (prudence or caution)." When I worked, I used "jolsok" rather than "sinjung." I doubt you will understand me, but I believe that was the right thing for me to do at the time, and for most instances, I used the latter.

Of course, there are times when you must use "sinjung," very much so, but at what cost? I always wondered. There will be no end to explanations. That is why I am going to tell you a story from my own life rather than pontificate further.

In the early 1970s, I was assigned overseas to the Middle East, to oversee construction there. What a bloody place!

In Saudi Arabia, there is a steel mill in the Northeast city of Al Jubail.

When we were constructing the steel mill, the company I worked for had to compete with other leading South Korean firms in order to secure the order.

Compared to other firms, we were much smaller, and the ordering organization had no interest in us. I knew we would fall even further behind in the qualifying round.

But to make matters short, I will start with the ending: we won the bid. We did not use trickery nor did we win over the others with sheer ability. If we were mentioning ability, we lagged far behind the others in terms of scale.

So how did we do it?

We used time effectively. We rushed to fill any type of contingency.

For example, say there was a question that the ordering organization had. Then no matter how complex it was, we sent a response in an hour. If it required further investigation or a longer response from company headquarters, we would set a date and say we would answer the question to the fullest by that date.

Our company's satellite office in the Middle East was not wealthy and we lacked some employees. However, the construction part I took full responsibility for. I would make a draft and use a Telex to send a response myself.

Telexes do not exist anymore; they were a type of prototype fax. During those times, we did not have fax machines and computers.

We would communicate via Telex several times, and the ordering organization started favoring us over the others, because of the quickness of our replies.

In most large organizations, there are many steps that one needs to take in order to make a decision or start something, and this would mean a delay of at least one to two days for our competitors, just judging by the paperwork required. This was, of course, assuming that the company was effective.

Why? Well, when a Telefax came in, they would have to stamp it with a received stamp, then it would go from the person who received it to the section chief and so on and so forth until approved all the way to the head of the department. Then after receiving a reply from one's superiors, it would come down the way it went up, then the reply would be drafted and sent back to the original sender.

But our company did not need this operating system. The sole person responsible was me. I would make the decision, draft the reply, then send it back. That is why the other company viewed the one-hour turnaround as nothing short of a miracle.

When we were starting negotiations, we went to the company that was responsible for making the bid offer, and they asked us about the nature of our workplace. How did it function so quickly?

I feigned ignorance as I replied, "Our company may be small and new, but in terms of speed and efficacy, it is renowned even back home. We have a different system compared to our competitors," I bragged.

My system was not normal, to say the least, and no wonder why they were curious.

Also, in doing business internationally, we had to take into account the time zones. If we got the timing wrong, then there would be a huge difference to make up. Even if our side was late by an hour and it coincided with the end of the workday for the company who would issue the bid, then it would be seen by the next day, or if it were a Friday, be delayed by two to three days.

Our two main competitors were both larger and had delivered in terms of results, but we used the time wisely and that is why we won.

The issuing company was Germany's Lurgi (now Lurgi GMbH), which was better known in the 1970s. It is a technology company operating worldwide in the fields of process engineering and plant contracting.

"Success and Failure are both subject to habit." So goes an Eastern European proverb. In order to succeed, we needed to change, starting with our small habits.

If you become a leader or manager of a company and are responsible for others, then you will notice that there will be subordinates who will bring in the work the next day, even if you hadn't issued a final due date the previous day. Small wonder why you yourself will like this subordinate better than the others and take more interest in him or her. If you use time wisely, then you will do well at work and be appointed to new positions.

The Art of Organizing

Go to your desk and see how many "pending" documents you have, and how many you have to leave as "pending."

After all, on your desk, besides the "pending" documents, you have many things that are unnecessary on it, such as other documents, books, and such. And probably, you will have odds and ends on it.

The difference between succeeding in the workplace and failing lies in the art of organization. When I was in the construction business, I could tell which teams were working effectively just by observing them at the site. The ones who did work without making a mess of the surrounding areas were the successful ones.

On one end, they may have been doing rough work, but the place where they hadn't started yet would be clean, and all the materials would be organized. These sites would abide by the due dates and the quality of the work would be top-notch as well.

Isn't this strange? If you have to organize, then this goes beyond just construction work.

It would require more hands and more work, and it seems like it would take longer, but this wasn't true. That is why organization is the key to success.

Presentations

In work, the ability to give presentations well is just as important as knowing another language. When you are a subordinate, you will need to give presentations to become the boss, then when you are a boss, you will need to give presentations to command your team. Like knowing another language, you will be able to use this skill like cash. You must train yourself to do well in the art of giving presentations.

When preparing your documents, you must depend upon them being a cut above the rest. If you use the documents I have collected over the years, you will have no problems. However, the rise of the Internet age has rendered them somewhat less helpful.

When you are about to give an academic presentation or an official speech, you must prepare the whole text. But a simple presentation giving one's opinion or teaching/preaching will be easier if you use notes. Instead of reading the whole speech out loud, it will reach the hearts of your audience members faster if you use notes.

A presentation that is intended to teach or instruct will be dry, and imagine if you were to just read from a piece of paper. Your speech will become a decree or a declaration. So depending on the audience, you must change how you prepare your speech.

The next step is to practice, but even if you are confident, I suggest a run-through. The more the better…it is better to practice in front of someone in a loud voice. The words that are tricky to pronounce, the words that are difficult to understand, will be fixed here, and until the rhythm and breathing is comfortable, you will also fix them here. I usually had your mother, Hae-June, listen to my speeches, and she was an excellent instructor.

On the real day of the speech, you have to pay attention to your posture and walking. Upon reaching the platform, you must present a confident aura as you stride across the stage. This should already be familiar to you as a member of this family. Of course, you will be a little nervous. But this part will be the first impression you make upon your audience, so it is very important. Do not drag your feet because you are nervous. Then you will have failed before even starting. If you give many presentations (lectures) and presentations of instructions, then you would expect to be less nervous, but I found myself getting nervous just the same. However, I did find that the more I practiced in advance, the less time I spent being nervous.

I will give you some tips.

Before standing at the podium, take several deep breaths. You must exhale for longer than you inhale. Then you must relax your muscles. Tense your shoulders then relax them, about twice. Then stride confidently across to the podium.

Once upon reach the podium, adjust the mike to your preferred position and rest your weight on two feet. Then place your arms on top of the podium and make a fist with your hands, then relax. Do this twice.

Do not clasp your hands together, but rather, have them rest upon both corners of the podium. If you do not have a podium, then hold your hands together. Do not place your hands on your hips or behind you. If this is uncomfortable for you, then weave your fingers together and make sure you are standing with your feet shoulder-width apart, then move your arms freely.

Some speech books advise you to see your audience as barley bags or pieces of rock, but I find this off-putting. You might feel at peace, but the speech will not be a resounding success. Do not look down on your audience.

During your speech, you must make eye contact once in a while. Do not make eye contact with just one side. Look at both sides, right and left, while modulating your voice and at just the right speed. Do not move your head quickly or make unnecessary movements. Gestures can be useful here, but I am not really adept at them. I advise you to learn about gestures from some other book.

In a speech, the draft (or text of the actual thing) is of utmost importance, and the second most important is delivery. It is the ability to express oneself, and I feel as though speaking well is similar to singing well. That is why you should practice modulating your voice. This training will serve you well, but can't be done in a short time period. You will have learned in the first grade how to read out loud, and articulation and intonation have only become even more important since then. You remember. So you must always practice your speech out loud.

Additionally, it is of utmost importance to modulate your breathing. Most people will be short of breath due to nerves before beginning their speech. That is why you should make a concerted effort to take long breaths as you advance up to the podium. This is one trick that will help you while public speaking.

Public speaking includes many things, but the things you should put into practice pale in comparison to having a go-getter attitude. During a lecture or review, or when there is a chance for you to talk, you should put forth your opinions. This is paramount to practice, and your public speaking skills will improve as well. You will also overcome stage fright if you do this.

Indeed, most times, you should be a person of few words and think before you speak, but never turn down an opportunity for public speaking. There is no need for you to put in flamboyant turns of phrase. There is a reason the lecture is needed. That is why the topic is and should always be one that has value. That is why you should prepare this in advance. If you do not have confidence in the topic, then avoid speaking all together. Otherwise, you will lose your bearings and lose your good standing in society.

Another aspect worth noting during public speaking is the ability to convey your thoughts out loud by presenting them.

The ability to write well is a trait that will serve you well. You can train yourself to write by writing daily diary entries; this should be sufficient. From elementary school to college, if you are able to write daily entries, then you will become a writer worth reading. If this is too difficult to put into practice, at least write once every two days.

The art of public speaking will not improve in a short period of time, and the ability to write well will take even more time. Therefore, more training will be necessary. I myself credit my habit of writing in a diary as the reason why I am able to write these words to you today, even though I am not an author by trade.

Being a Boss Is Hard

It is hard being the boss. You have to do well, so it is hard, and also because it is important, you have to do well.

The workplace starts with adults and adults are the ones running it, with the CEO at the top of the company's organization. That is why in this instance, the chicken comes first. To say that the egg came first is nonsensical.

For us, the day starts with the dawn, but for the Jewish people, evenings start their days. Of course, day and night, beginnings and endings are different depending on what you determine the start to be. So in the old, "Which came first, the chicken or the egg?" riddle should be determined by what you decide.

As mankind started with Adam, it must be that the chicken must have preceded the egg.

The crowing of the rooster at dawn has meaning, but the chicken egg remains silent. The world of adults, and the world of bosses, is, I daresay, important and difficult.

When I was head of the track and field division for the Asian Games and the Olympics, I placed more importance on the chicken rather than the egg, that is, the coach rather than the athlete.

The boss is in other words, both the key and the origin. The head of the household must do well in order for the rest of the members to be comfortable, and the leaders must do well in order for the country to accelerate into the next era.

In order to become a leader or boss, you must shine brightly from within. An aura of light should surround you, and attract those to you, otherwise, you are just an average Joe that even a squid (a euphemism for an ugly person in Korean) wouldn't follow. A leader must have followers. A leader does not necessarily have those who kowtow to him.

A leader should know that the subordinates are not to be handled or managed, but rather, made to follow. That is why a CEO or boss should "lead" rather than "bulldoze" ahead.

There is a famous infantry school at Fort Moore, Georgia in the United States where the motto is "Follow Me." That is why the hallmark of a leader, in my opinion, is his ability to attract many followers.

I say this time and time again, but if people do not follow in your stead, then you are not fit to lead. You will be anguished, and it will be a stain on society as well. I know that bad leaders are not punishable by law, but if society is to develop and mankind reach further than ever before, then the law should apply to bad leaders too. How many leaders have led people astray, leading companies to ruin and leaving people in tatters?

When I gaze at people around me, I realize that the failure of an organization, and the fall of a country lie in the failure of the bosses or the men in charge.

The reason why people go to pubs and talk badly about others is to really air their grievances, usually regarding their bosses. They would love to raise their fists in front of their bosses in fury, sometimes, in the faces of their CEOs or other high-ranking officials.

When we look back, even if a country like the United States has a former brilliant politician leading them, such as Abraham Lincoln, they are those like Hitler or Stalin as well. The ripples and storms caused by bad leaders such as the last two aforementioned ones, only serve to remind us of the importance of picking good ones. The situation becomes too dire if we do not, but mere words do not do me justice here.

Secondly, if you abhor responsibility, then you should never be a boss. You can draw and paint or start your own business and be your own boss. If you shirk responsibility and cherry-pick what is good... how stupidly selfish must you be. Isn't this a sin?

If a leader sins, then many people suffer and the organization fails, then society falls into a pit of endless despair, the nation topples, and the world becomes topsy-turvy. And yet, a person who is not fit to lead advances and says he will be the leader...is this not foolhardy?

If you are a member of this family, then I say without these two qualities that I look for in leaders, do not even think of becoming the boss.

Rewards and Punishments

When you are the boss, and in charge of many people, there will be some problems that you face almost on a daily basis. This is differentiating between public and private lives. The next are compensations and punishments. As I have spoken at length about public and private lives, I will speak upon the other issue now.

There is a story called, "qìzhǎnmǎsù," in Chinese. It means that Zhuge Liang was shaken by his beloved general Masu's combat failure, and had to behead him whilst crying.

This was meant for those who would follow in his stead, a type of corporal punishment so severe that nothing short of perfect would be tolerated.

But to make death the cost of failure? Was this really necessary?

One of the hardest things to do as a boss is to dole out rewards and punishments. A boss must reward accordingly for a job well done, and make the punishment fit the size of the crime, so to speak. That is why there is a four-character idiom called "xìnshǎngbìfá." This idiom refers to justly rewarding good service as well as justly punishing crimes.

In front of those who need to be punished, a boss will feel a lot of psychological pressure. If it is a matter concerning life and death, then the person in charge, how wretched must he feel? In the aforementioned story, Zhuge Liang beheads his favored general. How horrendous must he have felt.

That is why sometimes we argue over this very fable.

In my view, I wonder if Zhuge Liang's action had been too harsh. I think murdering a favorite general is bad, as a leader, unless he has led an insurrection or betrayed him. In the general's case, he had failed to comply with a direct order, but this was in no way threatening the kingdom's security nor had he had a secret desire to do so. He had really been trying to do better, but his abilities were not up to the task. That is why in this instance, I believe a discharge from the military would have been the correct course of action.

This is because extreme actions in my view, that "end" something, should be avoided. In issuing punishments, you should leave an impression, and this is really the most sensible thing to do. You have to give them a chance.

The reason why I mention this fable is because I, as a public servant, found it difficult to distinguish between private and public lives, and also found it difficult to reward and punish.

When I was the CEO of KEPCO, I tended to reward more than punish. As a CEO and boss, I believe that you must really give hope, give courage, and give them a fighting (and sometimes a second) chance.

In Wolseong, North Gyeongsang Province, the Korea Nuclear Power Plant stands. In the front lawn of the Plant, there is a monument dating back to 1985, which commemorates the world's best nuclear power plant (in terms of operating efficiency). Out of the five hundred (then) operating plants, Wolseong was the best that year. But as I mentioned in another book of mine, this was done with the blood, sweat, and tears of everyone who worked there.

In October of 1984, there was a mechanical control error at the plant caused by an agent there.

Most operators of nuclear plants need a long time to train, just like pilots who pilot airplanes. This is why most avoid accidents. But the operator had made a mistake, a human error. Luckily, this did not cause a huge accident, and the nuclear plant stopped on its own, but the plant had to be shut down for three months.

A nuclear power plant is different from an airplane in the sense that it usually has safety mechanisms that prevent it from total collapse. That is why the safety mechanisms are triple that of airplanes. That is why nuclear power plants are safer.

About a decade ago, the Fukushima Daiichi Nuclear Power Plant in Japan suffered an accident due to a tsunami caused by an underwater earthquake, but even in this instance, the nuclear power plant's safety system kicked into gear.

The problem really lay in a once-in-a-thousand-year event; a tsunami. After investigating, the researchers found that such a tsunami had not been seen for at least six hundred years.

The world may blame the Japanese employees at the plant, but probability tells us that this was a natural disaster and not a man-made event.

Let us return to the Wolseong case. The accident at the site was not normal. The damage to the company cost at least 80 billion KRW at the time and damaged our reputation and reliability. The company headquarters was in an uproar, and the South Korean government was also very worried.

The nature of the accident made it such that the head of the nuclear power plant had to resign immediately, and other executives and employees on site had to have their pay docked. On that day, I took another senior-level employee with me and raced to the scene.

It was as if the world was ending, as the mood was dark and icy. The head of the plant, as well as three hundred of his men, were hanging their heads. I did not know how to deal with this problem at first. Was I going to fire them or was I going to give them a second chance?

The head of the power plant was a graduate of the top university in South Korea and had spent many years training overseas. He was a top-notch expert. He was part of the "elite" troops of men at the company.

I gathered everyone in the auditorium. A heavy silence hung in the air. They all hung their heads, unable to look at me.

I started speaking slowly.

"A man can make a mistake. The problem is how to resolve the accident. You all have made a mistake and cost the company billions. You have a debt to the company. Repay the debt. I will give you a year. If you repay the debt, then I will not ask who is responsible for the loss," I said.

The auditorium was suddenly filled with whispers. They had expected the axe to fall, with resignations tendered and salary reductions galore. But what was this! The CEO had just said, "repay the debt!" Without a doubt, they must have cried out of gratitude that night…in secret, of course. And everyone who worked there resolved to work their hardest to repay the company for this sacrifice.

From henceforth, the nuclear power plant site was always electric with energy; it was like they were part of a fighting unit of troops. The head of the power plant, along with 350 employees, were fighting to resolve the stain to their names and became one.

A year passed. And they achieved the impossible: they set the benchmark for the best nuclear plant operator that year. It was the first time KEPCO had earned such an honor. This came about as a result of giving them a second chance, instead of firing them.

Stand Your Ground

When you are the boss, you are assigned with tasks, and responsibility also follows.

When you are responsible, then you have to see the work to completion. Then you have to know how to work well. But alas, no matter how high their marks were in university or how smart they were, it goes that few people are really good at their jobs.

This is due to two reasons. The first is the failure to get the timing right, and the second is a failure in perseverance.

I have talked at length about timing, so I will talk of perseverance now.

When you have spent time observing and working with many different kinds of people, you will realize that they all have their unique personalities and foibles. When the work is going well, this isn't a problem. But when the work hits a difficulty, they can fall into disarray. This is because everyone is different. This is what is called "junggunanbang," or all sorts of different opinions will issue forth if this happens.

When the person in charge does not stand his ground, then he is bound to fail greatly. There is a saying in Korean that goes like this: "A ship that slackens its sails heads up the mountains."

Grandpa also feels like a novice sometimes. But if you press me, I will say just this—the man responsible must stand his ground. The following words are what I did and are my personal philosophies on how to lead.

First, as I said before, think about the timing.

When everyone believes that "now is the right time to act," it means that it's already too late. When you are uncertain but you feel like the winds are about to change, this is the time to take action. Just do it. This is also called "sokjeonsokkyeol." Be as stubborn as a mule and stay resolute.

When you stay resolute, you will no doubt run into rumors that are spread by your subordinates, all the way down to the least senior person in the company. And no doubt the various departments and divisions may dislike your course of action. They all may act to convince you otherwise, to sway you in the other direction. But do not let this depress your spirit. This is what it is when you first start something new.

Do you know why? When you are a trailblazer, remember, others are not ready to follow, the company may not be ready, and you may be beset by mean words and complaints.

This is the first hurdle. You must endure, by closing your eyes tight and gritting your teeth, if necessary. You envision the blueprint, and you have it in your head.

It will be smooth sailing at first. This will make everyone happy, because it will have been easier than they anticipated, and they will start enjoying the work, perhaps even having fun. I myself feel buoyed. Everything is moving like clockwork, and everyone seems to clap for me.

But one day, a problem arises. It's past the midpoint or near the end. But of course. Because the job was easier than anticipated, they had gotten sloppy, and careless. The praises must have gone to their heads.

You have lost your grip, and wandered about, without concentrating on the task at hand. This is all too human. I say it's a human characteristic, differing only by degrees. That is why people should always take care to be humble.

That is why the CEO or the person in charge should foresee the hurdles before everyone else and persevere in the face of difficulties. Like I said, stand his ground.

This is a step beyond standing one's ground. You must push them to finish and persevere in the face of difficult times. It's not enough to endure, they must push ahead at all costs.

People will be tired. There will be mechanical errors or failures. That is why it's tough going, especially compared to the beginning. Some may despair. But I say now, that is why we don't just endure, we persevere.

This is what defines a true leader from the rest of the pack. A leader must foresee the hurdles and make plans ahead of them.

And when the hurdles finally arrive, he must unflinchingly rise, spur the mettle of his men, and even if the sky seems like it's about to crash around them, endure. Then keep going.

This is how one completes an important assignment, a job, a contract, etc. Grandpa's methodology may seem to some like stubbornness, but my successes speak for themselves.

Polish your heart as if you were polishing stone, smoothing it over and over. If you do this, you will see the way. If you continue to do this, however, and the way isn't clear to you, then it is best to heed the advice of your superiors and resign.

Who Is My Friend?

Dear grandchildren, let's say that you have a problem that keeps on bothering you today. Or there is a looming threat to your reputation. Who is the first person who comes to mind?

Of course, it should be your parents and your siblings. And who else? But of course! Your friends. But most people do not have friends that they can rely on when push comes to shove. You may think to yourself, "That friend, perhaps..." but when difficulty comes your way, most will shun you.

When you are in trouble, there are few who will help you in times of need. But if you are one of the fortunate ones, and have true friends, then you have indeed lived a life of success.

It is difficult to have real friends.

"Who is truly my friend?" Why don't you quietly ask yourself this question. Do you have any? Even if you don't, there is no need to despair. You can make friends. It's all in the effort. Friends to share the burdens or dangers that lie ahead, or even share joys are essential to a life well-lived.

"To live life without friends is to erase the sun from the heavens above," Cicero said.• But even if you don't take it to this level, Goethe once mentioned how essential friends were: "Every person needs a friend to lean on, and in his arms, find a place to express his sadness and even complain. This is why friends are vital."

In *Yijing*, a Confucian text, it mentions friendship as being like this:

• Marcus Tullius Cicero (BC 106–BC 43) left these words behind. Cicero was a Roman politician and philosopher, who wrote discourses on law and political theory. In addition, he is the author of some Christian theologies.

"Two people whose hearts and minds are as one can even slice a steel axe."

We live but once, and the biggest blessing is health, and the second blessing is the people around us and the degree to which they are good. Good parents, good teachers, good friends, and if you are lucky to meet any or all of the above, then you are blessed.

There are a great many people who are good in this world, and many accomplished men and women. Perhaps you will cross their paths at least once. If you live your life with purpose, you will find a good person to befriend. They do not have to be your peers. They can be younger or older, but if many hold them in high esteem, then age will present no problems.

You will sometimes find people who will awaken your soul.

Then how to pick friends, and how to go about finding them?

"When you first meet a person, take heed, as you would a thief. When you seek a wife, lower your standards by one measure, but when you seek a friend, raise your standards by one measure." This is a Western adage and warning.

When observing a person, observe his stance first, then his eyes, then his words.

When you consider these three traits, you will be able to sense his aura and his temperament.

I personally find that I prefer those who are not verbose. If you are unconfident about your judgment, then do not lose your temper. It takes time to know a person well.

"If poverty knocks at your door, then false friendships will leave via the window."•

• Words spoken by Wilhelm Müller (1794–1827). Müller was a German poet. His works include

"When excuses make slaves of you all, trials will test your servitude."••

You will realize if your friend was seeking a monetary windfall from his acquaintance with you or if he is a true friend who is ready to weather all storms with you, even the financial ones.

Once you have found a good person, you will need to cultivate your friendship as you would tend to a garden. Recall your past conversations with your friend. You will by no doubt be successful in maintaining a good relationship if you follow this advice.

Once you form a friendship, it should and cannot end with one misunderstanding, and likewise, the friendship will sour without putting in the work. Be aware that certain sacrifices may follow even good friendships.

"If your friend has only vegetables, gift him meat as a present." So says the *Talmud*.

"When you rescue a friend from a deep well, do not pay attention to the dirt on your clothes." This is a Western saying.

"You should not take as a servant a person who is stingy," Mozi says.•••

Without a doubt, it is in the small things. It is "jeongseong (sincere heart)" at work or a gift from the heart.

When you have time, you should console and encourage, and call your friend sometimes, and inquire about his comings and goings. Once every two months, you should dine together, and once every

The Beautiful Maiden of the Water Wheel and *Winter Wanderer*. The Austrian composer Franz Schubert put his words to music and both gained fame and recognition as a result.

•• From the works of Publilius Syrus (BC 85–BC 43), from his work *Moral Sayings*.

••• Mozi (BC 470–BC 390) was an ancient philosopher in Lu Dynasty during the Spring and Autumn period. That is also the title of the book, a compilation of his teachings and opinions.

three months, head for the mountains or partake in some other form of exercise together. If you are able, take a vacation together.

"If the stable collapses, then the cow will run away." Always take caution and fix the aspects that may not be firm with care. This again is jeongseong at work.

You should be able to confide your innermost thoughts with a friend, rely on him when able, share what you can, and share both joys and sorrows with him.

Discourage him from meaningless work, but if the work is just difficult and not meaningless, then help him. Do not slunk off, but work with him.

In the *Talmud*, it says, "Do not eat garlic by yourself." When dangers are ahead, fight with him, even if personal sacrifices follow. These traits define true friendship.

There is one other danger worth noting. You should cultivate a good friendship and avoid a bad one.

There are three types of friends. Friends that are like bread and butter, you will always need. Friends that are like medicine, you will need sometimes, and friends that are like the plague, you should avoid as much as possible. This is a Western saying.

For "Friends that are like the plague," do your best to stay on your guard. Enemies are not far away; rather, they are usually near us. "A declared enemy is preferable to a false friend." Does this Western adage not hold true?

Additionally, I would like to add that you should take care to not make new enemies. When you are excited about good things happening for you, and the rest of the group isn't as pleased, this can create enemies. When you attain a position of privilege that others do not have, you may have created new enemies without being aware of them at first.

In things you enjoy, take heed of the surroundings and be careful. When you are promoted, be humble and be generous. Even if circumstances do not allow you to be generous, surely a phone call will at least suffice.

A family event, you must always attend. Especially difficult events such as funerals require special consideration. As you rise up the career ladder, you will have to keep this in mind even more.

Some will be like bread and butter, some will be like medicine, and some will be like the plague. Distinguish between the three types of friends and behave accordingly.

"Who is my friend?"

From time to time, ask yourself this question. If you can think of one friend who fits the bill, then your life has been successful.

Grandpa would like to mention one anecdote that underscores the importance of friendship.

In August of 2011, Daegu, South Korea, came to host the World Athletics Championships. This biennial event ranks among the Olympics and the World Cup Soccer in terms of scale and popularity worldwide. However, South Korea is not as familiar with this event. Small wonder, as track and field events are not popular here.

Hosting the Championships requires an organizing committee by the hopeful host country, along with the government's foreign offices and nongovernmental organizations.

Remember the 2018 PyeongChang Winter Olympics? It took us three tries to get it.

In order to become the host of the World Championships, there is one pressing detail that can never be overlooked. It is whether track and field are popular in that country. If it is not popular, then there are no spectators, then no TV broadcasts focusing on the spectators, etc. The World Athletics (formerly the IAAF) council members put it to a vote.

Until Daegu, the World Championships had never before taken place in Asia, with the exception of Japan. China lagged behind as well; the council member from there could not even hand out his business cards.

But somehow, we achieved it. In a country that had no popularity in track and field events, and in the city of Daegu, which was not even the capital of South Korea.

So how was this done? Through my friends. On March 27, 2007, the twenty-five council members convened in Mombasa, Kenya, to cast their votes. The 2011 World Championships in Athletics, the thirteenth to date (back then) picked Daegu.

But how? In South Korea, a country that did not like track and field events? Yes, indeed. But how?

This is due to friendship. This is the power of "dongji," or like-minded people. It may seem like self-praise, but Grandpa's friends pulled through with my request. Of course, the bid committee, overseas organizations, the city of Daegu, the South Korean government, and the National Assembly all came together to design a plan of attack.

From 1991, I have been a council member of the International Association of Athletics Federations (IAAF). Now, the organization is known as World Athletics. I knew all my colleagues well, and likewise, they knew me well. Even Grandma, who has been a bulwark of support throughout our marriage, also played a role. In international events, everyone tended to bring their spouses, so Grandma of course played a pivotal role.

Council members were picked by over two hundred presidents of track and field organizations from all over the world. At the Congress, which convenes every four years, there are nineteen spots up for grabs.

There are a fixed six council members, by region, such as Asia, Europe, and Africa, who automatically retain their positions if they are regional representatives.

In order to secure the highly coveted nineteen remaining spots, fierce competition ensues. Not to mention that out of nineteen, six are automatically reserved for women. Small wonder why the competition was so fierce amongst my sex.

The tenure for a council member is four years. There is some turnover at every Congress. I am one of the few who were able to secure the council member position several times in a row. There are about four or five of us long-running gents from all over the world.

The competing host cities that year were Moscow, Russia, Brisbane, Australia, Barcelona, Spain, and Daegu, South Korea. Spain pulled out of the running, so at the final vote, it was narrowed down to Moscow, Brisbane, and Daegu.

In the final vote, twenty-three out of twenty-five voted. I could not vote for Daegu, so I had to bow out, and one of the council members failed to show up.

During the first round of voting, Daegu earned sixteen votes. In one fell swoop, Daegu had won! Brisbane had earned five votes, and Moscow, two.

I must mention now that if there is no clear majority, then until it is over 50 percent, the council members keep on voting.

When the results were announced, the council members expressed their surprise. The IAAF was also surprised. It was out of the blue.

In terms of council members, there are only about twenty or so of us (a total of twenty-five), so many were dear friends. It's difficult to support one over another. Usually, language unites the delegations, and whenever there is a problem the countries that share a language usually take over to moderate and resolve the issue.

The common languages are English, Spanish, French, with the English-speaking countries and the Spanish-speaking countries having more clout.

Since the atmosphere was like this, it was difficult to gain a majority. I strove to cultivate one-on-one relationships with people. This is why sporting international organizations may be difficult (for South Korea and other countries that do not traditionally speak the aforementioned languages).

As I have always said, I looked at the person and made a friend (or not) accordingly. I tried to pick those who had similar goals in mind. I was the lonely Korean speaker amongst the group.

When the voting was over, everyone stared at each other, at a loss for words. You? And you? Voted for Rocky?

That the world athletics family was surprised to say the least is an understatement, especially for a largely unknown city like Daegu. It had won over more well-known cities like Brisbane and Moscow.

We call this a fortuitous accident, or "yibyun," in Korean. But this was no yibyun and was no miracle. It was a person's heart. It was heart speaking to the heart. It's what Grandpa has always talked about… acting from the heart, jeongseong. Friendship overcame national boundaries and surpassed rational understanding.

There is one more thing worth noting here. Let's backtrack.

I did have some reservations. I did think that years of friendship may contribute to my friends believing that Rocky could pull it off. I did not mince words. I said, merely, "Daegu is my hometown!" These were the words I stressed. This kind of personal favor works between friends only. I could sense who would be on my side, by the firmness of the handshake.

But would my efforts reach fruition? I grew a bit nervous because of one thing: the IAAF (World Athletics) picked host cities based on several criteria, but one of them was, in truth, the popularity of the sport. This is all too obvious, and a good tactic. But my hometown of Daegu was up for the bid for the host city. In truth, I let my worries almost cloud my judgement and my good cheer.

Of course, the denizens of Daegu wanted it, but some difficulties that faced the city may have prevented us from winning the bid; however, we sorely needed the Championships to open here. As I stated before, though, this was just our predicament, and I did not expect anyone to give us more than usual once we received the bid.

Also, I feared that if Daegu was not able to pull off this feat in a spectacular fashion, then I was endangering my friends' goodwill and trust in me. How would they cope?

I worried. And thought some more.

"I have to find a justification. And the justification must fit the bill. I have to save my friends from losing face as well," I thought to myself.

So I thought and thought. And prayed and prayed. Then my prayers were answered in the form of a metaphorical lightning bolt.

"The World Championships in Athletics should take place in unpopular regions as well. Why? How much longer will only the popular cities host this event? Then we will lose the opportunity to grow our sport in unpopular countries. That is when more people will become interested in the sport of track and field. That is all," I said.

Ahead of the vote, this was basically the gist of what I said to the others gathered there.

My friends cheered for me. They slapped their knees at the logic. And without a doubt, they voted for Daegu.

Sometime later, Daegu pulled through. It was designated "The World Athletics City" by the IAAF. It became the second city to earn the title, after Stuttgart, Germany in 1993. Stuttgart is where Mercedes-Benz is headquartered. It is also the hometown of Hegel.

Chapter 6

Love and Marriage

●●

Men and Women

Some say that men and women are created equal. How nice. As we have progressed, it is only natural that men and women are equal. But the problem is that "equal" is considered "identical," and some people use these terms interchangeably.

Men and women may be created equal, but they are not identical, and there may be disparities between the two. The distinction between the sexes has been since Creation, and the two sexes have different duties and responsibilities.

Up until a certain point, a distinction must be made between the sexes. A female is female, and a male is male. That is why there is something to be said for traditional male and female roles, which keep order and peace.

When we say men and women are created equal, we are referring to the laws of the land. However, men and women cannot be identical with regard to everything.

What I have said now may be in keeping with the wisdom of the Universe. Of course, it must be God's Will. That is why we as human beings, cannot skirt the wisdom of His guidance.

In the West, thanks in part to the women's rights movement, they may face some trials and tribulations in the future. I daresay that some parts of the women's rights movement are flawed. Some eschew marriage and children altogether. Weren't females created for such a role? This is an extraordinary calamity.

We now turn to Japan, where an ancient philosopher named Toynbee once spoke.

He spoke at length about the necessity of making females desire to marry and give birth to children, for males are literally incapable of giving birth. This job of females must be made attractive, in the sense that women are born to this role of wife and mother. In fact, the role of "mother" is so great and powerful that it should not be seen as a mediocre job.

Why would Toynbee have gone to such lengths? I say I do not agree with all that he is saying. He calls motherhood "a job." That the role of the mother is a "job?" How can this be?

A judge or a pilot cannot be compared to the role of "mother." And the great honor of being able to give birth, that we relegate to the mere occupation that can be compensated by money, is absurd to me.

Who is singing in Heaven, and who will harvest the fruits of thy labor?

In the *Talmud*, there is a saying, "In the beginning, God created Man and Woman. But He did not create Woman from the head of Man, because Woman cannot rule over Man. Likewise, He did not create Woman from the feet of Man, because Woman is not a slave to Man. He made her from the ribs of Man so that Woman is next to Man's heart."

Children! Let us not quarrel over whether men and women are created equal. Instead, each makes the other whole, by compensating for their differences.

Isn't respectful love, which is much more powerful than the power you gain through fighting, much more precious?

We make one universe by leveling our weaknesses with each other's strengths.

As the Sun is to the Moon, and the Land is to the Sky, Female is obedience and Male is love.

The Romance Is Over, and History Begins

Spouses

"Son, pick a woman with heart, like the gentle spring breeze, and a woman of good character. If she cheapens herself or is of the jealous type, do not marry her. If she likes gossip then do not even stand close to her. A greedy woman spreads something ill like infectious diseases. Avoid her at all costs. Look for a woman who has wit and humor.

I hope that you will seek a woman with above-average looks because you will be looking at her forever. It may be just a slight difference, but when beauty marries heart, how beautiful will it be when you gaze upon her face early in the morning, every morning?"

I have paraphrased a famous American industrialist here who gave his son these instructions for marriage. I agree with most of what he's saying here, but the last part irks me. Average looks, in my opinion, are fine.

This man's greed is in excess. Will waking up to a beautiful face in the morning be the be-all and end-all? You should look for someone who will bring you joy through her actions and her life with you, who may not necessarily be a beauty.

In other words, beauty is fleeting and is often incompatible with luck. There is a saying in Korean, "miinbakmyeong," which roughly translates to, "the fairest flowers fade the soonest."

Another phrase in Korean worth mentioning, "A beautiful wife may be abandoned, but an ugly wife, never." So said old sages.

"A beautiful woman is to be gazed at and is not fit to be a spouse."

In beauty, there must be spirit. Why don't we call this grace, as befits a woman.

Even a Western proverb says, "Beauty is only skin deep."

"Do not seek a wife at a party, but instead, seek one at the barley threshing." Thus says a Czech's proverb.

"Why do beautiful women only marry cads (nobodies)? This is because a wise man does not marry a beauty." Somerset Maugham• said something similar.

Beauty, education, hobbies...they should be of the average sort. You should look at her family. This does not necessarily mean seeking them from the upper classes or aristocracy. Do they have living parents and lots of siblings? It is even better if they have grandparents who are still living.

Remember, children are the mirrors of their parents, so observe the parents, and you shall know all about their children. If there is too much of a difference in social classes, then that may present a problem. However, if the woman's side of the family is less affluent, it is ok. Women should avoid men who are poorer, however.

Drinking, smoking...before, I have not forgiven, but drinking is fine. But in moderation! A tumblerful or one glass!

I would like to quote from the *Talmud* again, "One drink for a female is beautiful, but by the second glass, she loses her dignity, and by the third drink she becomes immoral, and the fourth glass turns her into a

• William Somerset Maugham (1874–1965) was a French-born British writer who wrote with much wit about contemporary society. His best works include *Of Human Bondage* (1915) and *The Moon and Sixpence* (1919).

walking and talking disaster."

I would prefer the females of the family to stick to wine. Avoid soju and whiskey.

Remember, we have a non-smoking policy for the females of this household.

I have pontificated long enough on this topic of a potential wife, so Hae-June and Hyo Jung must be worried sick because I have not mentioned potential husbands.

Is there a need for much discourse on the topic of husbands?

"Just bring me a man for you who is like an ugly toad." In Korea, someone like an ugly toad means a strong and fortunate person. This is what I advised your mother, Hae-June. If you catch a man who is like your father, so much the better.

Hyo Jung, regarding your husband, ask your Grandma.

Now we turn to a Russian proverb for even more wisdom. "When you depart for war, pray once; when you set sail for the seas, pray twice, and when marrying, pray three times."

Is this because marriage is a scary business? No. According to a Westerner, "Marriage, for men, requires the man to gamble away his freedom, and for females, it's like winning the lottery." Marriage is a stark reality.

"Through death, all tragedies end, and through marriage, all happiness ends." This was said by Lord Byron.• Marriage is but a stark reality.

"When a man and woman marry, the romance novel ends, and

• George Gordon Byron (1788–1824) was a renowned British poet who championed heroes and the freedom to exercise one's will. He greatly influenced European sensibilities during his lifetime. His most important poems include *Childe Harold's Pilgrimage* and *Don Juan*.

history begins," says Schubert.

Marriage is a reality. Yes, reality. It is not a novel. Vanity and lies (fiction) are intolerable in the sphere of marriage.

"History" records the truth. I do not need descendants who write lies.

Where Is Heaven?

Where is Heaven? It's where love resides. Where love overflows. Where can we find such a place on Earth? It's through the family unit.

Maternal love, paternal love, filial love, a love for grandparents…all types of love that is reciprocated by most humans can be found in the family.

Where else will you find a place where love overflows on this Earth?

For Grandpa, Heaven is on Earth. The house where Grandma and my grandchildren live represents Heaven for Grandpa.

All families should be happy. That makes Heaven out of the home. Who else would bring happiness to you? Your neighbors? Money?

A happy family starts with a happy union of man and woman. Happiness only requires love and health.

Love is made between spouses, and health follows love.

If you wish to be happy, love each other. Then the family home turns into Heaven.

A father is a roof, while the mother is the pillar of the house.

The roof must be strong, otherwise trouble may follow. The mother should be the one who sacrifices the most. Then the family will be comfortable.

"A benevolent wife keeps biological (blood) relatives amicable, and a wicked wife will shatter the bonds between biological (blood) relatives." This is found in the *Míngxīnbǎojiàn*.

"The reason why marriages can be unhappy ones is because the wife doesn't make a fence around her husband, and her husband only weaves a net." Jonathan Swift• supposedly said this. Could this be true?

A foolish wife believes a husband can be made. This is my opinion. It appears as though all the work is left for the husband to do, rather than the wife. A woman who receives a lot of love from her husband will never turn bitter and shut him indoors. A happy marriage and family are the responsibility of the husband. This is a warning to the men of this household.

"Sun Wukong held in Buddha's hand,"•• and as such, the key to happiness is in the palm of the husband.

A plentiful livelihood makes the wife smile happily, and behind the happy smile, love and forgiveness will blossom.

There is peace in the bountiful love of a husband for his wife, and the wife will make flowers grow in the garden of their love. If there is no harmony in the family, then do not blame the wife. If love is lacking, it is the husband's fault, as I have said many times before.

Also, note the behaviors of our young family members. If you blanket their sins and do not punish them, then their habits will grow only worse. Spare the rod, spoil the child. They need to learn manners on how to behave towards their elders and learn how to treat a neighbor like his own self. Good habits will form as they practice them, and etiquette will become the norm.

In relationships with parents, children are used to receiving. But is this a good thing?

• Johnathan Swift (1667–1745) was a British writer and clergyman. He left behind an impressive legacy during the rise of the novel in Great Britain. His best-known work is *Gulliver's Travels*.

•• Sun Wukong is a monkey character wielding magic in the novel *Xiyouji* (Journey to the West) written by Wu Cheng'en during the Ming Dynasty of China.

A person who only receives, who doesn't know how to be thankful, and who doesn't know the grace of God becomes a pariah without friends.

Parents should teach their children to eat well, be healthy, and receive excellent grades. Other behaviors that may detract from the delight the parents have for their children should be avoided and thus taught.

So what should we be teaching? Help them realize God's grace and give thanks.

Let us think for a moment.

On a birthday, what do parents usually do?

They stretch their already thin budgets to buy groceries. They buy presents. They throw them a party. Then what will these children learn? A birthday is to be remembered, but not a time for exercising their innermost desires.

For children, you should make the table laden with food, as much as you are able, and make sure they understand that birthdays are "My birthday and Mother's special day."

This will mean that Mother's Day will be celebrated several times a year. Treat her well. A single flower may do. Even this will make her eyes well with tears of emotion and thankfulness.

In the *Book of Odes*, it says, "Father creates me, and Mother raises me, so I am so very sad. Parents, you endured so much in raising me. If I were to repay the debt, then it would be as high and expansive as the skies above and be infinite."

When the husband takes good care of his wife, who is also the mother of his children, and the children remain respectful, then the family will overflow with love and become Heaven. Heaven has to be earned, for do you think it can be easily made?

"A family is a place of respite from the harsh realities of life, where all arguments disappear or are hidden, and blossom into flowers of love, and the large one will become the last and the small one will become the first. A home is a place where you can learn to trust and share responsibilities in, and a place to give and receive love."

This was said by Orson Welles.• As I have reiterated time and time again, is this not Heaven on Earth?

As Josephine either acknowledged the greatness of her husband, Napoleon, or not, in the family home the larger ruler becomes small, and vice versa. In our family, our two youngest grandchildren, Hyo Sung and Hae-Yeon, become large than life.

A father's love, and a mother's love, along with an outpouring of love from their children, create Heaven on Earth.

Crisis Management

A marriage may not be an apt metaphor. But the relationship between the spouses is like when a lonely wolf and gypsy start cohabiting.

If you always travel alone, eat when you wish to eat, starve when you don't have enough food, sleep when you wish to sleep, and move about when you wish you wake from your slumbers, is this not the life of a lonely wolf?

But starting from a certain day, being cooped up in the same place will start taking its toll on you. In the past, you may have been able to be an independent sort, doing and thinking as you please. However, in a marriage, you have to think of the two of you together, do unto him

• Orson Welles (1915–1985) was an American actor, director, screenwriter, and producer who is remembered for his innovative work.

as you would do for yourself, and even spend much time doing things together…so how awkward at first must be this union?

During courtship, men and women tend to see only the good qualities in each other. The fantasy of a romance novel ends when you get married. Sure, when you are dating, you make plans to meet for several hours on a certain day, both dress to impress, etc. This may as well be like acting because pretending is the norm of the day.

But starting from day one of a marriage, the veil from both will be whisked away. You dine together, sleep together…so small wonder why no one human can keep pretending for twenty-four hours each day.

You will see for yourself what the other has been hiding from you. You will inevitably see more faults. But of course. You have already seen the good.

No wonder why starting from day one, a married couple may start fighting. Some will fight loudly. Some will inevitably shatter their marriage ties themselves. I worry for the young people of today, because of the high divorce rate.

Grandpa loves and likes Grandma so much, and yet, we fought constantly throughout our marriage. It was strange to go a day without fighting. As the ancient sages of Asia used to say in ancient times, this "love fight," or fighting because we loved each other, was common.

In the early days of a marriage, it is normal to fight. It is not unusual. You will fight because you are uncomfortable, because you cannot keep your temper, because you are angry, and because you love each other… small wonder why it's strange to not argue at all (I'm looking at you and your husband, Hyo Sung).

The best solution is to fight well. What do I mean by this?

A fight between lovers is like slicing a blade through water. It does not leave a mark. If you throw plates, then it will require you to buy another to replace them, and if you break a window, then it is detrimental to the neighbors, and if you fight with your fists, then you will leave marks, and if you say barbs, then you will leave bruises on the heart…all these things leave marks.

The men of our family should take this into account. To leave marks is the work of a fool. Of all these, take caution with your words. Sentences that start with "You always…", for example, are at the root of many arguments. What is always, anyway?

Another point of contention in a verbal argument is "You never… not even once." All of you must guard against these words.

Both sentences may even start with the word "dangsin," or the Korean word for "you" which is often used between married couples. The problem is that after this affectionate word, you attach your spouse's weaknesses to it and attack him. It requires pointing out the other person's weaknesses. It has always been there, but you've just noticed it.

That is why if you are on the offensive, you feel betrayed and angry, while the recipient of these words becomes hurt, because you are speaking the truth.

When you are fighting with your spouse, avoid truths.

"Get engaged with two eyes open but marry with one eye open." Isn't there such an adage in Korean?

In any case, avoid injuring the other person with harsh words. If you breach their trust by pointing out their (true) faults, you will leave a bruise on your spouse's heart.

But do not go so far as to avoid fights by enduring the pain. Otherwise, it will fester like a deep wound and cause disease.

Fight. But do not leave any trace of fighting afterwards. This fight is always going to turn you into a better person.

Additionally, do not fight for the sake of just winning. I have found no good men (or women) among those who fight until they win the argument.

To me, it makes no sense. What will he glean from winning an argument against his beloved? In a horse race, do they not say that winning is a shameless and brazen thing to do?

The finale of an argument must be the husband hugging his wife. Whether he was right or wrong. There is no embarrassment to be found here. What kind of man wants to win over his beloved, anyway? It is undignified of him.

In the game of dignity and integrity, when it is all over, do your best to honor the other person.

"Do not make a woman cry. God counts every teardrop that she spills," the *Talmud* says.

Slicing Water with a Sword

The worst thing to do in an argument with your spouse is to leave home. At the very least, you have to go just as far as the front yard...do not go beyond this.

You shouldn't kick the neighborhood dog either, but when a man gets into an argument, he will have the tendency to burst. Do not clutch the steering wheel of a car when you are very angry. Keep this in mind.

When I was young, whenever a fight started, I would run away. This is one strategy. At any mention of an argument starting, I would retreat elsewhere, outside the family home.

Every time I did this, Grandma would adamantly block the door, and refuse to let me leave. This would cause an even bigger fight. But she was obstinate. She stopped me many times. Sometimes it really was my fault, but I did not lose my strength; rather, I lost my nerve due to her iron fist in a velvet glove, so to speak. She never retreated.

For a long time, I did not know this. But as I grew older, I realized the wisdom of Grandma's ways. If my obstinance led me away from the family home, then the next day would become even more dangerous. She knew this even when she was in her twenties.

When you are angry, think of this strategy of Mao Zedong: "If an enemy comes, you retreat, and if he retreats, you advance."

A fight will usually start with one person taking offense. If two start fighting at the same time, then both will suffer wounds. If the other starts speaking then retreat a pace or two. If this doesn't work, then say, "Wait! I think I did something wrong."

You may not actually have done any wrong, but you say this anyway. That is why this is a tactical strategy and maneuver. Most problems can be handled once you say this.

But the nature of fighting is not always logical.

There will be times when you are at your wits' end. When you feel this way, do not hesitate to fight. Otherwise, you will develop an illness. Fight. Fight well. But do not leave marks. Remember, you do not want this to become a long, drawn-out battle.

Do not let the fight extend into tomorrow. This is the hallmark of a bad person, who has no right to do this.

But there will be times when this doesn't apply. Then direct your anger at an object. Some may even call this wit. An empty bottle, a plastic container…there are many.

But throw them in the front yard or on the floor. If you throw it at another person, you are not a part of a family. You have no right. Even this tactic should not exceed once or twice in a given year.

And if this doesn't work, then retreat. Avoid the other person. The next room is ok, and the living room is fine, and remember, sometimes the best tactical maneuver is to retreat. For this is as tricky and dangerous as a minefield.

But the best way to end a fight? Get up and hug your spouse hard. Direct the anger and let it concentrate in the arms; the more viselike the grip, the madder you were. You should take comfort and hug your spouse.

Hard!

If you use words at this time, you will be disqualified.

The Stairway to Heaven

"White snow is slowly piling up on the onngi…"

This phrase is from the first letter that your Grandma penned to me.

"If I, Rocky, could love a deity (God) it is through my love for you."

This is how I expressed my feelings for her for the first time.

I was a little bit shy, so I used the God metaphor. And because I was shy, I could not say it directly to her but wrote it in a letter. The letter is old and faded yellow now, but Grandma still has it for safekeeping.

The first time I held Grandma's hand was at a backstreet of Deoksu Palace, in downtown Seoul. The first time I held her in my arms was in front of a movie theater at Ewha Womans University. These places I hold in my heart as treasures.

There used to be a set of stairs in Mt. Namsan where I would take a walk. There used to be a coffee shop called "San Yu Hwa," named after a flower. It was near Taegye Road. I would traverse these steps while holding Grandma's hand. I used to regard this as the stairs to Heaven. It's a pity this place doesn't exist anymore.

Love is beautiful and sad and great at the same time. Love can be pain, sadness, or mercurial and subject to moods. A love between a husband and wife is all mighty yet changeable. If you fail to pay attention for a little while, the other may start pouting. If you think about your spouse and are kind and considerate, the love comes back to you tenfold. The love between man and woman can make Heaven, but sometimes the love begets an argument. That is why marriages need to be cultivated, like a garden.

Grandma would be washing the plates and I would hug her from the back. Or I would call her spontaneously. On my way home, I would buy a flower and give it to her when I got home. I would put a love note on top of the dresser unbeknownst to her. At any possible moment, I would say, "I love you."

These instances represent love between husband and wife. And you will find that love always takes effort on either end.

This is the stairway to heaven. Did you think that there was another route?

Do you know why grandchildren are so adorable? It's because they change. They may be smiling one minute, and walking on their chubby little legs the next, and call me "Grampy!" when they see me.

Hae-June was always the prim and proper one. She would say "Grandpa!" most succinctly. But poor Hyo Jung, she would say, "Grampy." From one day to the next, grandchildren change, and this brings about an everlasting love for them.

Love is the same. It must change, wittily (one hopes), and tender loving care will deepen the love and make it blossom in our hearts.

There is a term that we are all familiar with: the "honeymoon." According to the Oxford English Dictionary, it means "a delectable time," but in this book, I would like to compare it to a waning moon.

The metaphor refers to married couples.

As such, married couples may compare their love to a full moon, but as time passes, it will become smaller and smaller, until even the crescent disappears. This is the chimerical nature of love between spouses. Keep this in mind.

Grandpa and Grandma these days have nothing to fight about. Are we just tired of fighting? No. There is no need to brandish the sword and slice water with it. There is no reason to fight, so does this mean our love has cooled? Not necessarily.

The real reason why married spouses fight is because they do not know each other.

As Grandpa, I love Grandma so much, and she doesn't know...she doesn't know because I don't know how to tell her.

That she does not know how much I am working to please her...it's not that she's unaware of it. She just doesn't reciprocate with actions.

As such, this will bring about a fight.

The other reason is because both won't back down. Even if we start fighting because we are unwilling to understand each other, if one person gives in, then the fight will resolve on its own.

But when you are young, as I once was, it is not easy to back down. That is why fights start.

Now Grandpa and Grandma know each other so well. One gesture, one glance, and we speak a thousand volumes with one look.

Someone broke a vase. A very expensive one. In the past, I would have yelled, otherwise, like a disease that starts festering in one's heart because of anger would have taken hold of me.

Of course, the antique vase is very valuable. And yet, it's already broken, but if we hurt each other's feelings, then would this not be even more of a tragedy?

Likewise, the person who broke it and the person who witnessed it will understand somehow the feelings of the one who threw it initially.

I know what Grandma likes best.

On a day off, have a cup of tea in the living room with the sun warming the both of us. In this instance, words are useless and become cumbersome.

Grandma gazes at me, and I at Grandma. We say a thousand words with one glance. And we repeat what we've said so many times:

"I love you!"

"You are so handsome!"

Chapter 7

The Children's Education

A Person's Character Is Formed in the Home

A Father's Persistence

The Adolescent Years

Love and Example

A Person's Character Is Formed in the Home

What happens when a person does not receive an education?

He becomes a Beast.

What is the most important out of all types of education? It isn't found in most textbooks; it is on how to be human.

According to Mencius, an ancient Chinese philosopher, if "one cannot sympathize, one cannot feel shame, if one cannot be humble, and if one cannot tell right from wrong," then he is not human.

This is an excerpt from his writings.

Human dignity, self-awareness as an individual, the ability to distinguish between goodness and lies, make rational decisions based on what is right and wrong, and finally, to seek out what is beautiful and avoid the ugly...this is what it means to be human.

If children are to learn at school, in subjects like math and history and physics, then I think a person's character is formed in the home. From my vantage point, I say that if they're well-mannered, then I do not set such store-by-book learning.

It's good to have an education, but he should be a gentleman; the same goes for ladies.

What separates Man from Beast? Intellect and the ability to "know thyself," as Socrates once said. This is a lesson that spans generations.

A long time ago, Hyo Jung was watching a borrowed VHS tape of *Cinderella*. She had borrowed it from Hae-June.

She watched it intently until the scene where the stepsisters tore at her mother's repurposed gown, then asked, "Grandpa, why are they tearing at her clothes?"

No matter how many times I tried to explain it to her, she kept on asking. "But why?" and "Because of what?" I grew weary.

Hyo Jung was only three years old at the time, so small wonder why she did not understand jealousy.

In my mind, the toddler Hyo Jung's confusion only added to my grief. In her kind toddler Snow White-like self, where could I find hatred and goodness and moreover, evil?

I am the type who does not believe in the Good Nature Principle (xìngshànshuō) or Evil Nature Principle (xìngèshuō).

When a person is born, he is endowed with a snow-white heart. It really is a beauty, as it is both good and virtuous. I believe that a person starts off as a tabula rasa. What is added or subtracted from him depends on what he is taught and what he learns.

What sets a person apart from other animals is that it has a growth period. At the age of eighteen, he becomes an adult, and his schooling would have taken at least twenty years in order for him to fully form and contribute to society.

It is a blessing that a man, from birth until he leaves his parents, has a long time to become the person that he is. He receives both an education from his parents and school.

I am of the opinion that "book learning" and learning a technical skill can always be done as long as the person is assiduous. But the lessons that one learns at home can never be learned once a man leaves the nest. Therefore, parents, while they are still living, should instill in their children good manners and habits. Remember the Korean saying that a three-year-old's habits last until his eightieth birthday?

There are those who are like the salt of the Earth, and light up their environments wherever they go. These people have received a good education at home. They are honest and modest and yet confident. They have a good aura about them. They are the pinnacle of a good education that they have received from their parents.

That is why the task is up to the parents to cultivate a human being who is of good character. This is the duty of all parents.

Prenatal Education

Then where does education from home begin?

It starts from the womb. Our ancestors used to say this. But in truth, it should start even before he is a fetus in the womb.

Grandpa has reiterated at length in the previous pages that a family should be like Heaven. A healthy and loving couple, with enough material wealth that they do not endure poverty, should eagerly await the arrival of their little one and regard him or her as a blessing. This is the environment where a child should be conceived.

Before the advent of Christ, in China, during the Zhou Dynasty, lived a good and wise king named Wenwang.

There are records of his mother giving him a prenatal education.

In the *Sohak*, it says, "She was of a constant and unchanging nature, solemn and hard-working, and only did good deeds. Once she fell pregnant, she did not look haughtily at others, did not listen to noisy sounds, and from her lips fell no arrogant words. Once Wenwang was born, he was bright and precocious, knowing a hundred things upon learning one thing, and became a great and model King."

A person's education starts from the home, and this anecdote is a testament to this fact. This tale is from over 3,000 years ago. I bow my head humbly at the ancients' wisdom.

When you are pregnant, if you feel anxious or very tired, it will affect the fetus. You should regard morning sickness as a blessing, rather than a curse, for this affects the baby as well, according to some studies.

There was an American study some time ago that tracked a hundred women who had "problematic" children. It turns out that 60 percent had someone in the family who committed suicide during their pregnancy or had marital difficulties.

In South Korea, we have teachings called "The Seven Prenatalist Doctrines," or the "Chil Tae Do." This guide is first and foremost in the world, and its teachings are excellent.

The First: Do not climb high, even onto a stool, and do not traverse rough roads or cross ditch water, nor cross a fence or escape through a hole meant for dogs.

The Second: Do not talk too much, or laugh loudly, or be startled, or be frightened, or cry.

The Third: While sleeping, sleep upright, while standing, stand straight instead of leaning on one leg, do not see anything dirty or impure, and do not listen to lustful sounds.

The Fourth: Do not eat chicken (it may give you goosebumps), do not eat duck (it may cause you to walk with your feet splayed), and abstain from eating squid, as it may soften your bones.

The Fifth: Read the writings of old sages and read beautiful poetry.

The Sixth: Keep close to you and collect those that are high and mighty, such as turtles, phoenixes, jewels, good scents, and norigae (a traditional Korean trinket).

The Seventh: Do not have an appetite for the sensual, lose your greediness, and do not complain or allow jealousy to fester in your heart.

In one of Thomas Mann's novels, the mother listens to Baroque music for the benefit of the child in her womb. The child, who has listened to the music from the womb, once born, becomes a kind-hearted and trustworthy person.

These days, many pregnant women listen to music as part of their prenatal preparation. They say that listening to Hayden and Mozart create happy-go-lucky children while listening to Beethoven and or Brahms create serious children.

Hae-June, your English and English poetry astonish everyone around you. You have never even majored in English.

While your mother was pregnant with you, Hae-June, she used to memorize an English poem in the evening, and prayed that the baby in her womb would become like Princess Diana of Wales (she was a fan, as were many back then and still is today).

When your mother was pregnant with you, Hae-Yeon, your mother thought of Yi Sun-sin, the great general, often. That may be the reason why until you were five years old, you refused to wear skirts and always wore pants. When visiting me and Grandma at home, you used to skip and play and simulate war games.

I was very happy to play with you, my youngest grandchild. Hae-Yeon, you have brought me a lot of joy in my twilight years.

But these days, Grandpa is a bit concerned. After becoming a fine young person, you spend most of your days with your nose in a book, studying. I sometimes have to stop you from over-studying.

Hae-Yeon, do you not remember the phrase, "gwahyoobulgeup" in Korean? This refers to too much being just as bad as too little.

Childhood

Until you go to kindergarten or perhaps even nursery school, your mother is the one who raises you and teaches you.

I feel like this is the first hurdle in a series of important ones. Because this is the time when you start drawing upon the tabula rasa that is your temperament and personality.

According to psychologists, a person's personality is about 50 percent formed by the age of three, and by the age of five, about seventy-five percent of it is set for life.

"Personality is destiny," so says a Korean adage. This is true, a hundred times over. A person's personality dictates his friendships, study, whether he will succeed or fail, and even his health. Is not a mother's duty to her child so very important during these early years? I believe it is.

In old songs, they sing of a mother's wisdom and pity her straits, and likewise, a mother's responsibility is a heavy burden.

Do you now understand the reason why I do not like women of this household having jobs after giving birth?

After becoming a mother, who can allot the time towards working, when she has a baby and husband to care for? And indeed, is she not responsible for child-rearing, and the child's early education? It is all in her hands, and she will have so little time to spare for a career.

Even if you can only afford two meals a day, please be a stay-at-home mother until the child goes to middle school. That is why the man of the house is then responsible for his family eating three meals a day, even if he is the sole breadwinner. Being a father and a husband is not just about pomp and circumstance; rather, this is why a woman should worship her husband like the gods above.

If your personality is your fate, then what kind of personality should you have?

A bright and sunny temperament, who is active, brave, and big-hearted…there are many examples of good traits to have but all in all,

I wish for the child to be bright. Bright as in not dark. When all the world order, in his view, is bright, then he will be good, but if he is dark, then wouldn't he starve?

If you are bright, then you will smile, and if you are moody, then you will probably be frowning. A person should be of a sunny disposition.

What is a sunny disposition, anyhow?

An optimistic outlook, a belief that everything will turn out fine, not despairing despite any negative circumstance, and striving despite it all.

What must one do in order to become a brighter person?

It will be through the mother's love. Through a mother's milk, her bright laughter, her whispers of love, and her pats on the back.

It is better to sing a lullaby, even if she is a terrible singer than to have children listen to audiobooks at night.

All mammals in their infancy need their mother's care. Even lions and tigers and even dolphins adhere to this rule.

In the early nineteenth century, many babies in Europe died of "marasmus." In Greek, it means to "wither away."

This is another old (but true) tale…long ago, in New York, a famous hospital was puzzled as to why so many of the one-year-old infants in their care died. The hospital's reputation suffered, and it became a cultural issue. A doctor finally came up with a solution: to have nurses cuddle and hug the babies in their care.

Until the child is five, the mother should take the utmost care in taking care of her little one. She should hug him, pat him on the back, and whisper to him that she "loves him." When the child starts speaking and understanding words, she should always praise and be in awe of him.

The mother should read to her child, rather than have him listen to an audiobook. Even a mother's clumsy singing will be better than any fancy singer.

One aspect worth noting in a child's care: take care to instill his habits early on. Honesty, respect for one's elders, saving rather than spending, the ability to keep promises, manners, and leaving nothing on one's plate…etc. The mother should always teach her child how to clean and tidy up as well.

A "human" education that one receives at home is all for creating a good and healthy person. It does not necessarily mean a sage or a great person will be made. A bright and sunny disposition, who is thankful for everything, thankful for his parents, and thankful for the skies above him and the ground below…if a person has a good temperament, then he will be thankful for all.

What is the opposite of giving thanks? It is being beholden to someone. Being beholden to one's parents, to society, to a friend, to the skies above and the ground below…it is not knowing how to be thankful.

"Carve your indebtedness onto stone, but your good deeds, into sand." These wise words were said by our Korean ancestors.

Out of all these qualities, one must take a special interest in honesty. Honesty, in this instance, must encompass a healthy person and a healthy people…which will result in a healthy nation. This is the most basic of rules.

Other healthy habits include rising early, drinking water before a meal, having set times for going to the bathroom, etc.

As they say that a person's habits start from the age of three and last until his eighties (or even later), form good habits now. Manners may maketh man, but habits can have far-reaching consequences on many things, such as one's health.

If a man's personality dictates his destiny, let us remember that a child's future depends on a mother's education.

The Boyhood Years

A school should be where one exercises one's mind and trains one's body. In particular, some criticize schools and say that they do not provide adequate moral education and are lax in teaching what it means to be human. I think otherwise. I think education on how to be human should be relegated to the home; the parents, and not the teacher, should be held responsible.

How can someone learn how to be human from another person if he has not learned from his parents, who have been living with him for almost twenty years?

Of course, there are excellent teachers, and there are times when we reach realizations due to them. But I feel as though this happens upon a person reaching maturity. In order to behave as a person should, the task rests solely on parents, in my opinion.

A mother's education is important during the early years, but a father's role looms large during a person's childhood while he is attending school. A boy will develop reasoning skills, and intellect, and learn, and grow taller, and grow muscles. A mother's gentle touch may not be enough to keep the child in check during his boyhood; hence, it is the father's responsibility to keep him in check. This is not just because he is physically stronger than a mother, but it is because he is the father.

While reading, I realized that there are many things that fathers have to shoulder during the education of their children. I am of the opinion that when a person becomes a father, he must provide for his family. At the very least, give them three square meals a day. However, remember not to overburden him.

If a mother is responsible for a child's moral education, then the father is responsible for teaching the child good behaviors. How to make friends, how to train one's body, how to study, and keep within the social norms…these behaviors are the father's to teach (outside of the home, of course).

How can a busy father do all these things? Do not fret. When the child is young, play with him. When he gets a bit older, play sports with him. Hiking, tennis, fishing, etc…all are good examples. What is important is that you can do this together.

I am particularly fond of tennis. Everyone in the family can play, and lots of others also play tennis, and it's easier than golfing or skiing. I feel as though tennis is one of the best cardiovascular exercises one can do.

According to research from Harvard University, a person who plays tennis well has to calculate the ball's distance and speed, and anticipate its direction. It is one of the sports where you use your brain, so I recommend it highly. If you start playing as a child, then you will make good use of this ability in the future, and the whole family can play together.

Another important way a father can bond with his child is through conversation. As much as you can, spend time talking with your little ones. Aren't there so many topics to discuss? About man's bravery, great men's sacrifices, and hard work, the history of humanity, the mountains and the ocean, of all things beautiful in this world…

If I only impart the paraphrased wisdom of Confucius here, you may become a dull man. So, talk of other things as well; your friends, how you fought with your enemies, a teacher you dislike, about mother and her faults…this will help you avoid becoming a stubborn, dull man.

"Scoop water from a round bowl, if the container is square."

This phrase is found on my father's gravestone as an epitaph. This was his basic tenement for life. In all things, do not rush, but take time. Moderation is key. Relax.

My father passed away at the age of seventy-three, in 1967. I have seven brothers and sisters, and I am the youngest of his sons (the seventh child). He had me when he was forty-two, so I was treated more like a grandson than a son while growing up.

When I departed Daegu to take the entrance examinations for Korea Military Academy, in 1954, my father drove me to Jinhae. I was already a young man of twenty.

In Masan, he spent the evening with me and the following day for lunch, bought me ox bone soup. Even after we bid goodbye, he stood for a long while, waving…over sixty years later, this memory is etched deeply in my memories. I long for him still.

Ox bone soup may be common now, but back then, it was an expensive delicacy.

Time magazine is read by over 120 million people today in print and digital form, according to its current Media Kit. One of its founders, Henry Luce,• was the son of missionaries in China, and he once spoke of spending some time in the Shandong area.

"Before dinnertime, my father would take me on a walk outside of the village grounds. And sometimes he even treated me as a grown man, while discussing history and philosophical problems with my younger self."

Spend time with your children, discussing all manners of things. A father does not exist just to earn money for his family.

• Henry R. Luce (1898–1967) was an American magazine magnate who founded *Time* magazine in 1923 with Briton Haddon. In 1930, he founded *Fortune* magazine, and in 1936, *Life* magazine. Luce was a luminary of the magazine publishing world and helped cement *Time* magazine as one of the leading news publications of the day.

It is not an easy task to be the breadwinner of the family. And I know fathers are busy. Are there any who aren't?

Once a week, take a walk together and play tennis, and twice a month, dine together and eat bulgogi.

The *Talmud* says, "Parents who do not teach their children are like parents who hope that their children will become thieves [in the future]."

Why do we talk to one another?

I am not here to impart only the wisdom of Confucius. I am not even saying we should make famous tennis players of the children. This means that during childhood and adolescence, a parent should nurture their child's dreams.

In the East, there is a saying, called, "ipji." It means setting a goal for your life. A child will act in accordance with his goal, and this will impart meaning to his life. Without it, he will be aimless.

When one mentions today's teens, many people lament. But adults are to blame as well, for they are sometimes deplorable. This all boils down to our fathers' responsibility or lack thereof.

Fathers should play often with their children and spend a lot of time talking with them. Topics for conversation can include hopes and dreams, training one's body, intelligence and knowledge, social mores, bravery, and sacrifice…the list goes on. Additionally, fathers should also impart wisdom regarding sacrifices not just for one's family, but country.

A Father's Persistence

A father is usually the breadwinner of the family. He is also the sky to one female, his wife.

How much authority he has! This encompasses children's education and appropriate punishments. But alas, the elders' authority has seemingly vanished today.

In every aspect of society, there must be elders. That is what will keep the order. This is what society should be like.

Sometimes the father doesn't measure up as an elder.

The smallest unit of society is the family, and yet, if the father loses authority within the family, all types of catastrophes will result. Authority must be earned, it is not a right.

A father must be self-aware, and regard fatherhood as a duty. He has to act like a father.

I will not pontificate on how a father shouldn't behave. But let me tell you one thing. A father is persistent. He should set some rules and make sure the children abide by them. These can include greeting older personages first, not lying, and keeping a curfew. He should also teach his children not to talk back.

As I said before, authority is not a right. A father must show a willingness to be a good human being, be resolute, and be confident… these are the qualities that make a father.

A long time ago I chanced upon a Japanese student movement memoir.

Here is a paraphrased excerpt:

"Today's the day. I bid farewell to my father at the front door. In my heart, there is a battle against government authority and the established order. There is a gush of hostility in me and a willingness to fight. But the shadow side of me that lies deep within, makes me wonder to myself if I am doing the right thing. I have some skepticism about what I am about to do."

"Inwardly, I wanted my father to firmly restrain me from what I was about to do. But instead, he merely said in a weak voice, 'Son, be careful.'"

I was shocked by my father's attitude and felt like someone had dumped cold water on me. I felt despair. I ran out onto the road. I fought like an angry ghost. I fought hard, with my life in the balance.

In the early sixties in Japan, Japanese universities were rife with riots, so much so that they put ours (Korean) into shame. Even the prestigious University of Tokyo shut its doors for a year and made all students repeat a year later.

When you are a father, do not hesitate to strike your child with a wooden rod.

According to the *Míngxīnbǎojiàn*, "When you love a child, hit him with the wooden rod often, and if you hate the child, give him lots to eat."

In the Holy Book, I remember a phrase…it referred to taking up the rod or spoiling the child.

The Adolescent Years

In a child's education, this is the period that is most difficult for parents.

A child will become rough, and be combative, and have a mercurial temperament. If the parent prefers things to be neat and tidy, then he will be messy on purpose, and if you stress manners then he will be rambunctious, and he will fight and get punched in the eyes, resulting in bruises, hitting the family dog…you will be at your wits' end.

But do not shrink with temerity. Everything is a testament to the child growing up. It is like weathering a storm that everyone has to go through in order to become an adult. But the difference lies in how you will respond to your child when he acts like this. If you confront him openly, he will only be recalcitrant. At first, you must realize that your son or daughter is not normal.

It will require trickery to win over your adolescent child. It's as complicated as Chinese martial arts. You have to retreat first. This will require patience and wisdom. You must retreat one to two steps then strike. If you do not do this, then you will end up hurting each other. It will cause a rupture in your relationship that is hard to mend because it will scar him.

It is the same with your child. Teenagers are rough…remember, have patience and understanding and you will reach some kind of realization on how to resolve this situation.

At first, take his side. Even if he did wrong, wrap him with loving kindness. After a day or two, scold him. He will already be repenting, having regained his senses. This will return your child into the kind person that he always was. The work you put into your relationship with your child will inevitably show, as love will be a backdrop to your reconciliation.

When I was posted to the Middle East, your dad, Hyo Jung, and your mom, Hae-June, had to leave me and Grandma to study elsewhere. They did not spend most of their tumultuous adolescent years in our loving arms…when I think upon it, how wretched they must have felt in a foreign land (the Isle of Wight in the United Kingdom).

It pains me to this day. So Grandpa also does not have the authority to speak about this subject. I am not the one who was uprooted, sent overseas, and had to attend school elsewhere. I will refrain from saying more about this subject.

In everything, there are principles and rules. I will mention some of the most important ones here.

First, a father should not chastise his child.

During the adolescent years, it is natural for a child to rebel. He may say he knows not what he does, but that is a lie. He knows he will be scolded, and knows he did wrong…in some instances, he wants to be scolded so he commits an act of indiscretion. And logic won't work here. It's mere stupidity to rationalize his behavior, both on his part and yours.

When I was young, in school, the most rambunctious child was the one born to a family whose members worked in Education.

It may be better to pick up the rod…but then again, it's just as poisonous to say, "When I was your age." It's like pouring gasoline onto a fire.

If your child commits an act that is hard for you to understand, then gaze at him through narrowed eyes. You should not talk at this point. Your face is angry, but still, very much alive.

Call him once, then narrow your eyes at him again. He, who has expected a beating and receives only a cold and narrowed look instead will start feeling remorse. But then again, a fist could fly out at any moment, so he will have some trepidation in his heart.

When he committed the act, he will already have been filled with regret and his conscience will be bothering him. Anxiety, fear, sorrow… these complex emotions will have gripped him to the core. About five minutes is enough to issue forth such emotions from your son. Then call him to you, address him by some putrid slur, then say, "Come over here!"

He will come as if he was willed by a magnetic force. Then you will slowly rise from your seat and hug him tightly. Your arms should be viselike. Do not speak. This will only last a minute. During this minute, the child will be filled with relief, thankfulness, and other complex thoughts.

"Go to your room." You have understood his heart, then shared the same hurt. There will be times when your son cries in your arms. Again, refrain from speaking and hug him even tighter. Then stroke his hair or pat him on the back. Finally, he will feel better.

"Go to your room."

Second, do not meddle.

During adolescence, a child will take interest in the opposite sex and will be filled with curiosity.

Parents will be anxious and read letters and even eavesdrop on the telephone. To put it bluntly, you may be wandering up and down the hallway while your child is on the phone. You have to remember he is different from when he was just a child. He wants to create his own world. He no longer relies on his parents for everything.

Not meddling is a science, useful for raising children as well as dealing with employees. You must respect his world, and if you meddle during this time, even the kindest of your children will turn on you. Most people want to hide their problems with the opposite sex; this is basic human psychology at work. If you read his love letters, spy on the phone, etc., your son might burst with anger.

If you start trying to control your teenager, he will start lying to you. If he starts lying about what he's up to with females, then some kind of big tragedy will occur. Don't spy on him but do set boundaries. You must also observe him carefully; every movement, his clothes, his phone calls (the frequency of them as well as who is calling), the letters, his comings, and goings, and who his friends are…keep silent vigil. Afterwards, make your final judgment.

There will be changes that are different from those he or she has exhibited before. Are there changes in her grades? Friendships lost or regained? Or some guy causing her heartache?

If you observe carefully, you will be able to figure out the situation and the cause of the situation. That is why you make a plan to fit and address the situation. If you start berating your son, and saying, "What has happened?" it's already too late. You must consult his teacher and or a doctor. Leading a young man is a difficult plight, and even with one's wisdom, it may all be for nothing. You may not receive a direct answer from the doctor or the teacher. In the process of consulting them, you may arrive at the answer yourself.

The times have changed, as have some of our societal morals. I have little faith in this topic. But some of the big "rules" I believe should be followed even in these trying and dangerous times.

First, your children can only date after the other party has been vetted by the parents.

This does not mean some are ineligible right away, it just means that before officially dating, your teenager should bring his girlfriend home to meet you and his mom. Dates should take place in the home...either ours or theirs.

Second, you must stay a virgin until marriage. This is non-negotiable for children in our family. This is not up for debate. Follow this rule, as it is a family rule.

Sex education is necessary and good. A parent may do it, or an educator. It depends on the situation. If you are to stop them from engaging in behaviors that are too adult for them, then you must be firm by explaining why.

This time is when your teenager's heart will be bursting with a newfound joy. He will grow into his manhood, and his muscles will begin defining themselves on his biceps, and he may just kick at the concrete fence just to prove that he can. The tons of energy that will accompany your boy's rise to adolescence and eventual adulthood means that he will have to find a source in which to use up all this energy.

Unfortunately, Confucius' teachings pale during these times. It will not do to discipline him with such teachings. Instead, encourage him to engage in sports of all kinds: fencing, judo, rugby, American football… etc.

Chivalry is not dead, even upon reaching adolescence. And he should participate in group sports. Tennis he should have taken up during his elementary school years, so he will have grown in skill by this point. On the weekends, as a parent, play singles. You will be able to exercise as well as converse, thereby killing two birds with one stone.

You should also, as a parent, encourage club activities such as mountain climbing and marine training.

A more difficult method may be going on an overseas trip. About two or three people, including your teenager, should go. An itinerary and going during a school vacation are absolute musts.

When your Dad, Hyo Jung and Hyo Sung, was in the United Kingdom, I sent him on a trip to Rome and back. On this trip, I made sure he had limited funds. In Korean, it translates to "penniless journey."

Grandpa made your Dad go alone, without boarding and deplaning an aircraft. Instead, I wanted him to travel via buses and or the railway. I did not even give him enough money for a hostel; instead, I wanted him to experience real hardship. I wanted him to sleep while traveling on a train or bus. I only gave him enough money so he wouldn't starve to death.

Dad suffered a lot, Hyo Sung. Or so he says. During the early leg of this trip, for two days straight, he took trains and transferred to a bus. Meals consisted of a single slice of pizza or a hot dog.

This "penniless journey" or "mujeon yeohaeng," is different from the backpacking trips that are more popular today. The content and the end goals are different. A backpacking trip is for sightseeing, but a muh jun yuh haeng allows one to experience poverty.

A round trip fare for trains and buses only, and barely any money for food…this is exactly what I had in mind for my boy. There were no extra funds for anything else, and he had to travel while basically starving, otherwise he could not return to the United Kingdom.

Hardships experienced while young you would even pay to experience, as adults may say. Do not shy away from pain and hardship. Without hardships, a person cannot grow.

Love and Example

The basic tenement of education is love and example.

Lessons that are not accompanied by love are equivalent to a person without a soul. Without a sense of example, an education is like a sandcastle upon the sand. Some sages have said, "The king becomes everything to his knight, and a father becomes everything to his son, and a husband becomes everything to his wife." All education must start with love and a sense of example…otherwise, everything I have conferred throughout the previous pages becomes like a promise written in the sand.

As with everything, timing is of the essence, so you should take care not to miss important milestones in a child's education.

"A life's plans stem from childhood, and a year's plans are found during springtime, and the day's plans are formed during dawn. If you do not learn while young then you will know nothing when you are old, and if you do not till the soil in the spring then there will be no harvest to reap in the fall, and if you do not wake up with the dawn then there will be nothing to do for that day," Confucius said.

With respect to children's education, we must face head-on, where to begin and what to teach. This is a problem of selection, and how much, is a matter of degrees, and the ultimate purpose is where to set the end goal. This methodology is not limited to just education. This can resolve just about any problem that arises in this world.

When I have a problem, I always think of the principles and the lessons it may hold. The fundamental principles are in books, while the lessons are in history. If you are the sort that doesn't care for rules or lessons, then at least get to the heart of the problem. If you figure out what the problem really is, then you should be able to arrive at an answer. If you still can't figure out what the answer should be, approach it from the opposite perspective. If this course of action fails as well, pray. Pray hard. Prayer always gives me strength. It has always helped me find the thread that would unravel the problem that I was pondering.

When I first left my son at boarding school, I was preoccupied by a slight problem: I did not wish for him to smoke. As many of his schoolmates smoked in high school, I wondered if he would fall victim to peer pressure or become enchanted by the idea of smoking like a "cool" teenager. How was I supposed to stop him from smoking? When he lived overseas? How could I spy on him? I couldn't stop him from smoking if he chose to. And like the frog in the old Korean fable, he might just take up smoking if I kept on lecturing him, Hyo Jung.

"It's fine if you smoke. But you must tell me when. Your pocket money is sparse already, and I have to know if I should wire you more money for cigarettes," I said, as I left.

Back then, the boarding school that your mom and uncle, Hae-June and Hae-Yeon, were attending was very strict. They had to comply with strict regulations regarding leaving the dorms and they had a curfew. They even set a limit on an allowance, so parents could not give their child more. I believe it may have been around fifty pounds…so about ten pounds per month for a whole semester. I remember your mother, Hae-Yeon, loved to buy Cadbury's. But alas, I doubt the pocket money was enough for either your mother or your uncle. From your father, Hyo Jung and Hyo Sung, I did not hear a peep from him for the whole semester, until the next school break. From thenceforth, he has not picked up a cigarette, Hyo Sung. Had I said to him, "If you start smoking like those kids over there, then you will get stupid and it will harm your health and it is costly and does more harm than good. You shouldn't smoke," then maybe the situation would be different today.

Grandpa used to wash the feet of both your father and your aunt, Hyo Jung, until they finished college. Sometimes. I would prepare a basin with a towel and heat the water in a teapot. They would tentatively extend a foot when older, but when they were younger, they would get so excited. They got so excited that sometimes they got scolded for it. When they got older, I could sense a change. A hesitancy. They might flinch a little if I touched their feet. I was sorry and thankful…and I wonder if they still remember now, like in the Good Book, how I used to wash their feet. The bellyful of love that I felt for both, and they for me, I could sense from my fingertips down to my hands.

The fundamental essence of education is love.

Chapter 8

Manners

Manners Are a Form of Affection

Manners in Society

Manners Found in the Classics

Manners Are a Form of Affection

"Manners are a form of affection, and they are not law."

A mentor of mine that I highly respect to this day said this to me once. When I kept on insisting, "manners are the law," he had kept quiet for a long time. But eventually, unlike his usual self, he spoke firmly and would eventually prove me wrong.

How could manners be a form of affection? For a long time, I did not and could not understand.

Confucius says, "Manners speak to the truthfulness of the heart," but I found this argument weak.

Well, I am of the opinion that manners speak to what a person can do or not do in relationships, and is agreed upon by law. They are unspoken promises.

You respect your parents, you recognize your elders as elders, keep the employer-employee relationship, and keep the laws of the land as we cohabit on this Earth, and abiding all these things can lessen friction between parties…this resolve must be what my mentor was referring to. But this seems like it falls under "law," rather than "affection."

In Korea, since the days of old, we were referred to as, "The country of courteous people in the East," by the Chinese. Even the proud Chinese people saw Koreans as a mannerly race.

In the classics during the Later Han Dynasty, the Chinese admonished those who had lost their manners and directed them to go to the

East, to learn manners. What had happened to their race? They had turned into barbarians.

From the days of old, our country has been handing down the tradition of manners, that even the Chinese were impressed by our teachings.

You may refer to some of our old classics, such as *Naehoon* (manners in the home), written in 1475 by Queen Sohae, wife of King Seongjong of Joseon Dynasty, Yulgok's *Geokmong Yogyul* (manners for children) written in 1577, and Lee Deok-moo's *Sasojeol* (Book of manners and self-disciplines) written in 1775 during the period of King Jeongjo of Joseon Dynasty.

When you have time, if you encounter these books, you will realize the wisdom of our Korean elders and will learn many old tales and learn to appreciate the wisdom found in antiquity.

Some do not understand my love of the classics. Some harbor ill will towards me, for my high regard for the Chinese classics of old. I do understand their predicament. It is toadyism. However, sometimes we need to disregard where it comes from, to be truly wise.

Most of our studies, in my view, that we learn are about 90 percent from the West. The root of the Humanities is from ancient Greece and Rome. However, I am of the opinion that since we did not have the classics as China did, for example, Korea loses face, a little bit. When we acknowledge what is good and great, and hold them in high regard, this becomes wise modesty.

When we read the classics, however, we should heed the words of old sages...especially in comparing then and now (what I mean by this is the situation at hand). There are words that will not be fit for the current times. But it is not wise to eliminate these words altogether. This is akin to saying that since Galileo's heliocentric theory was proved right,

God's words in the Bible are wrong.

If you misread the classics, then you will lose the original spirit of what they meant, and may wander down the wrong road. You should take heed not to do this. Even our Korean ancestors once justified their incorrect actions to persuade public opinion and wasted time by misreading them.

Once I began writing this book, I kept thinking of my old teacher, who had said to me, "Manners are a form of affection!" I finally understand what he meant. I've experienced some odd moments with this teacher. In terms of our cultural heritage, he is a giant of a man, and yet, he is a man of slight frame. Additionally, he is as warm as the spring breeze, but I wondered how he sometimes seemed as dangerous as a boulder.

Even now, when I treat him to makgeolli, or traditional Korean rice wine, because he does not wish to go anywhere fancy, I do not question why he said some things while drunk. I still hold him in high regard.

My teacher was warning me against regarding the classics so highly that we take them word for word, and literally. A person's soul could get ensnared in old traditional values that have no meaning in today's times.

My teacher's name is Kim Young Tak, and his nickname and nom de plume is Gu-yong.•

So he was right, after all, a hundred times over, in saying that "manners are a form of affection."

• Kim Gu-yong (1922–2001) was a poet and scholar who was born in North Gyeongsang Province. He studied Buddhism and Korean Studies. In 1953, he graduated from Sungkyunkwan University and taught as a lecturer at Korea Military Academy and as a professor at his alma mater. He also worked as a translator, translating works such as *The Three Kingdoms* from Mandarin into Korean. In 2001, he won a prestigious literary award of South Korea.

Manners in Society

First and foremost is dress. Isn't there a saying that "clothes make the man," or "clothes are wings?" Clothing and all manners of attire are important in society and the workplace.

Clothes probably originated out of a need to keep out drafts and shield oneself from rain and wind, but now cars are readily available and we have high-rise buildings and the standard of living has risen. Thus, clothes take on an additional meaning, a decorative as well as a functional one.

Your clothing in the home should be different from the clothes you wear when you are going out, whether it is to work, to a party, to the gym. Remember that clothes should have a functional as well as decorative aspect.

Your clothing should not clash with its various aspects, and you should develop a sense of style.

You must dress well, and for the occasion, and to your budget. Expensive designer clothing is off-limits. If it is too dressy and over-the-top, you may end up looking cheap.

Your clothing should be beautiful, and do they not say in the West that there is a harmony to be found in clothes? That is why for the occasion, and the color, and for your budget...all these elements must come together when putting together an outfit.

Of course, there may be colors you are particularly fond of, or designs, or accessories that you like that will define your unique sense of style.

Sometimes an expert may be consulted to help you with this.

Of manners in the workplace, in public, or on trips abroad, I would advise you to consult other books.

In terms of personal relationships, such as greetings, introductions, visitations, invitations, gifting, and more, I would refer to Hyo Jung and Hyo Sung's mother's etiquette book that I mentioned before.

There is one aspect of society and manners that I find sorely lacking.

This is regarding the nation's flag and the nation's anthem and the head of state. In terms of the head of state, like the president, they seem to be doing an OK job at different events thanks to emcees. But in terms of the flag and the anthem there are still many things to be taught and learned.

Examples include how to venerate the flag properly and how to behave when the national anthem is being played.

One way to learn is to, once a year, observe Korea Military Academy's weekend parade. This will provide ample opportunity to learn how to venerate the country's flag and the nation, and observing the formal parade will give you a chance to reflect on your country.

When Grandpa first enrolled at Korea Military Academy, it was located in Taereung. I remember the day clearly; it was July 1, 1954. Nowadays, it is called Hwarangdae, Fort Hwarang, located in the Seoul Metropolitan area, but back then it was a part of Gyeonggi Province, and called Taereung. The name is derived from the tomb of Queen Munjeong, the mother of King Myongjong of the Joseon Dynasty.

Back in early 1954, Korea Military Academy was in Jinhae, at the southern tip of the Korean Peninsula. As the Korean War broke out in 1950, KMA, located in Seoul, was temporarily closed and reopened in Jinhae in January 1952, this time as a four-year institution. This was during the height of the Korean War, and the capital, Seoul, was the battlefield overrun by the Chinese army.

To this day, I am surprised and proud of my KMA predecessors. That they were able to establish the Academy during wartime was and is still astonishing.

During this time, the second lieutenants of the army were called "expendable." This referred to them being easily replaced, discarded, or used up, like bullets or cannonballs. The death toll for platoon leaders was so high that at the height of the war, they would often return as a corpse as soon as they reported to the regiment commander and went up to the hills to fight. As the death toll was so high, the training for officers was only three months long, at the most, and when pressed, lasted only a month. These were terrible times.

Koreans must remember the high cost of this sacrifice, and that the Republic of Korea was established on such grounds. That during these difficult times, a four-year university that would produce military officers was established is food for thought. It surprises me to this day.

The summer of 1954 at Taereung was scorching hot. Upon enrolling, for two months, we cadets had to pass "Beast Training." This training treats people like animals, and the training is so difficult that it is hard to put into words. Some are unable to withstand it, some dropout, and some die of accidents. Every year, about twenty or so did not make it.

When I think back upon it, it is a sin to lead someone to his death. That a person can break during training, and not even during real combat, is, in my opinion, a lack of foresight.

There are sometimes health reasons, such as a weak heart or lungs, that contribute to a potential officer being unable to pass training. That they would misspend the golden days of their youth and die as virgins…is this not a sad consequence of ill health?

Grandpa survived. During the brutal training, I sweated about half the sweat I would during my entire lifetime. I cried so much that I must have used up all my tears.

During training and while at the Academy, I vowed my allegiance to the country that I could die for. Strangely enough, Grandpa misses those four years, and am proud to this day to call myself a military man.

Manners Found in the Classics

South Korea joined the 5030 club in 2014, the seventh nation to do this in the world. This club refers to over 50,000,000 for its nationals and when the GNP per capita is at least USD 30,000 per year.

South Korea also hosted the 1988 Seoul Summer Olympics, the FIFA World Cup in 2002, the IAAF World Championships in 2011, and the 2018 Pyeongchang Winter Olympics. This puts South Korea in league with developed nations, as it has hosted four world sporting events. Can Koreans even go so far as to suggest that just by national status or cultural heritage, it can enter the ranks of the top ten developed nations in the world?

Unfortunately, in Grandpa's opinion, I disagree. I am sorry. Why? I have spoken repeatedly about people who lack a certain social pedigree—in terms of being honest, following a moral code, and keeping and having manners. I am of the opinion that many of our countrymen are not up to par when compared against these parameters.

We do not need to travel far to find our "betters," for lack of a better word. Japan is nearby. Do you understand what I am trying to say?

Because of our two nations' fraught history, we are sometimes frenemies with Japan. But I am of the opinion that we need to learn the good aspects of the Japanese and recognize them via what I have dubbed as "cultural magnanimity."

At the very least, we should recognize their love of manners and tradition, caring for others, cleanliness, etc…and try to absorb these qualities as well.

Rather than boasting about our GNP per capita, we should focus on becoming a nation and a people that is admired and respected by the world…and take heed to look back at our past blunders.

The world order of today seems to be dictated by powerful nations, and their hegemony extends beyond logic. We are all seemingly adopting a Western methodology to everything, from social practices to government and economics. This is because they are wealthier and much more powerful. This is not grounds, however, to say that our Eastern minds and cultural heritage should be pushed aside by adopting all the Western conventions.

The reason why I venerate the classics is because I know firsthand our great cultural and scholastic heritage. I am of the opinion that these should be the foundations. Then, we may add Western conventions and knowledge to them. This will help our nation keep up or even surpass them.

The zeitgeist of the times is Western, but their customs and ways of conduct should not be copied in full; we should marry them with our once-upon-shining customs and ways of conduct. If we do this, then we will create well-rounded people and command respect, even from the West.

There are many books on Western etiquette, so I will focus more on our Korean conventions in this book.

Hae-June, Hyo Jung, then let us take a look at our Korean forefathers' wisdom and knowledge.

A Well-Rounded Education

In the East, there is a notion that a person must learn, from the very beginning, starting from the mother's womb until death. In the *Sohak*, there is talk of "taegyo," prenatal education, which I have explained in the previous pages. But the book also contains what a person must learn, by age level.

These include reading, math, archery, horse riding, learning poetry, music, and dance. All these form a "well-rounded person." These teachings are full of deep wisdom. Even if you find them boring, I believe you should read them and learn them by heart.

"When your child learns how to feed himself, then teach him to use his right hand, and when he starts to speak well, teach your son to respond quickly. For a daughter, have her reflect on her response and answer more slowly. For a boy, give him a pouch of leather to hang at his waist, while a girl should wear a purse of silk."

The pouch or purse is really a small pocket called "ban" in Chinese, and a boy should use one of leather and a girl should use one of silk. This denotes the characteristics that our ancestors wanted each gender to have; a firmness of manner for the boys and beautifully languid manners for the girls.

"When the child is six years old, teach him how to count, and directions (N, S, W, E), and when the child reaches seven years of age, make sure that he cannot sit with a girl, and they should not eat together. When the child is eight, upon leaving or sitting at the table, make sure he eats after the elders lift their spoons; this teaches them manners. When the child is nine teach him to count the days."

A famous phrase in Korean, "namnyeochilse budongseok" means that a "boy and a girl should not sit together after they have reached the age of seven." Of course, this does not abide by the spirit of the times.

But to just ignore this wisdom from the ancients and attack this is foolhardy. As I have said before, when you are learning and processing the wisdom of the ancestors, you must make their teachings fit. You cannot just literally read the words and not wonder at the historical significance of each sentence. You have to read the zeitgeist of the times."

"When the child reaches his teens, he should learn music and memorize poetry." To paraphrase, at the age of thirteen, he should learn to be flexible, and at the age of fifteen, he must prepare to become a husband.

"When he is twenty, he will learn to dance gracefully and learn to refine his manners even more, and wear expensive silk clothing and armor, and learn to protect and defend his King."

"Upon the age of thirty, he shall take a wife, and act like the man that he already is, and study widely and extensively, and be humble with his friends and honor the Emperor's wishes."

Here, the "act like the man that he already is," means receiving some land, taking part in government affairs, and going out into the world.

"To receive land refers to, at least during the Zhou Dynasty, the state-owned land that was distributed to each farming family, or 10,000 pyeong, upon marriage."

"Upon the age of forty, he will receive a government post, and do well in his work with his ingenious mind, and present these ideas for the good of the country and the Emperor, and if the servitude to the Emperor is not to his liking because it does not align with the Good, then quit and leave the post."

"At the age of fifty, he will receive a title and become a boss, and rise to the position of a government official, and take part in political affairs, and at the age of seventy, will retire."

Here, the resignation refers to stepping back in a government post. Is this not a fitting end to a "whole" education?

Early on, Greece's Plato introduced the concept of the "Philosopher King" and the education that he ought to receive. This education is just as good as the one I wrote at length about here, demonstrating that the East and the West are both able to produce and cultivate men of talent.

Table Manners

This is an excerpt from *Gokrye*, a book of detailed etiquette regarding how to behave during ceremonies or events.

"When dining with others, take care not to eat until you are full, and do not wet your hands. You should not ball up the rice, take big spoonfuls, and do not drink from the bowl directly. You should eat without making slurping noises, not bite into bones, and not return meat that you have already started eating back to your plate. You should not throw the bone to the dog, not eat all of one dish prepared for everyone, and not blow on your rice in order for it to cool so you can eat it quickly. Do not eat millet with chopsticks."

"With soups that have various seasoned vegetables, do not drink just the broth, and do not add artificial seasonings to it. Do not pick at your teeth at the table, and do not drink the brine of pickles. If the guest has to season his soup, apologize and say that the host was unable to get the flavor right, and if the guest drinks the pickle brine, then also apologize."

"With wet meats, use your teeth, but with dry meats, do not use your teeth to cut them. With bulgogi, you should take small bites."

In the *Sasojeol*, there is a saying that everyone should share the food, regardless of class.

"If a special delicacy unexpectedly arrives, even if the portion is small, divide it amongst the old, the young, the distinguished guest, and the poor; if you give everyone a taste, then a spirit of goodwill flows forth from all."

"When eating sashimi, take care to not sneeze when you are eating daikon, and do not cry either. Do not eat so much daikon that you burp at the other person."

"When eating lettuce wraps, or rice wrapped in seaweed, do not use your fingers or the palm of your hand, because they are unclean. Instead, use your spoon to make a small ball of rice, then use your chopsticks to put one to two condiments or appetizers on it, then place one or two lettuce leaves or seaweed lavers on your spoon, then have it enter your mouth. You should take care not to make this too big, otherwise, it will not fit. This latter behavior is against common courtesy."

Is this not detailed and caring?

"When eating, be careful, and carefully eat meat… do not suck on the bone, do not chew on the bone, and do not chew on the drumstick of quail either. This is because there is a chance that the bone might splinter. Do not rip off meat with your teeth. This is because the juices will stain your clothes. Do not mix your rice with marinated crabs. This is behavior common to the destitute."

"While you are eating, do not make unnecessary noises. For example, when eating daikon or pears or chestnuts, do not make a crunchy sound, and when eating noodles or drinking soup or eating porridge, do not slurp, and when you are drinking water, do not make gulping noises. In general, when you are eating, you should eat slowly, but not so slowly that it appears as though you do not wish to eat, and do not eat so quickly so that it appears that the food may be taken away soon, and do not toss chopsticks unto the table, and do not make noises with your spoon whilst eating."

What do you think? Is this not comparable to Western etiquette but even more warm-hearted and perhaps even a cut above it?

In the *Sasojeol*, there is mention of drinking and how one should go about it.

"When you are drinking with your elders, when the wine is brought to the table, you must go to where the wine is and bow and receive it. If one of your elders does not let you do this, then the younger person must return to his seat, but if the elders have not finished their drinking, do not start drinking until they have finished."

"Even if the spirit is very strong, you must not screw up your eyes and say, 'ka,' while breathing out and you must not drink too quickly, and you must not use your tongue to suck on your lips."

Even now, some lovers of the drink, when someone says "ka," punish him by making him down another drink. But do you know where this practice originated?

Manners of the Body

In the East, there is a phrase called "zhǎngyòuyǒuxù," which simply means "elders first." Having elders as guests is one of the five important principles in Confucianism and these manners have been preserved; is this not a beautiful way to behave?

If there is a twenty-year gap or more between you, then the other person by no doubt old enough to be your father; thus, you can address him as "zunzhe," or a "precious person," and if the person is over ten years older, than he is old enough to be your brother-in-law; then address him as "zhangzi," or a "superior person."

If a person is close to you in age, or only a little bit older or younger, then the first is called "shizhe," and the one who is over ten years younger should be addressed him as "xiaozi." The first means "fittest person," while the other means "small person." Anyone who is younger than you by twenty years is called "youzi."

If you see the complexities in our traditions of old, and how developed they are, you can delve enough further. As I have already mentioned, there are five levels of relationships and the ways of greeting the other person are all different.

If "zunzhe" is off to start on a long journey, pay him a visit and bow. This is called "ci." When he has returned from his long journey, then you must pay him another visit; this is called "jian." When he goes to a happy occasion and bows to an elder, this is referred to as "he." When someone has performed goodwill towards you, and you go to pay your respects and bow, this is called "sa."

Not only this, but there are rules of etiquette regarding where to receive the visitor, whether it is a room, the living room, the garden, or the front gates. Additionally, it changes depending on which class of honorifics you must use. For example, when "zunzhe" is being sent off on a long journey, one has to walk about a hundred steps or more from the main gate to say farewell, then return. Is this not the height of manners?

In *Liji*,• one of the Five Books of Confucianism, it says, "The nobleman has a relaxed composure to his face and is very careful, but he pays respects to those who he meets on the way if he is a man to be respected. Then he adopts even more manners, in order to be careful. He makes his footfalls heavy, and his hands, modestly composed, and his eye movements are neat and tidy, and he is careful with his

• *Liji* is one of the Five Books of Confucianism and contains rules of etiquette and manners, and their defense of them, that have been around since the Zhou Dynasty.

speech. When he makes a sound, it is in a quiet tone, and his breathing is careful. His posture is straight, and his face conveys a certain solemnity."

Does this not surpass today's modern manners?

In *Gokrye*, a book of detailed etiquette regarding how to behave during ceremonies or events, it says, "When sitting next to someone, do not extend your arms outward, and when you are giving something to someone who is standing, do not hold them in your arms in an embrace, and when you are giving something to a child who is sitting, do not give it to him while standing."

When entering the living space, make some noise by saying something loudly, so that they can hear you from the inner rooms, and if there are two pairs of shoes and you hear voices talking, then go in, but if you do not hear anything then do not enter. When you enter the room after opening the door, your gaze should be towards the floor, and the door latch should be held with two hands. You should not look around hastily at the room, and if the door is open, then keep it open, and if the door was shut before, then shut it again. If there is someone behind you who is about to enter then you should close the door halfway. You should not step on someone else's shoes, and you should not take another's place. Raise the hem of your pants or dress then enter the room and go to a corner of the room with a quickened pace, and you must avoid replying.

Manners in Speech

The *Sasojeol* warns against speaking too much.

"A person who is talkative runs into many dangers, and lessens his 'jeongseong,' or sincerity, and he ruins his luck and his work comes crashing down."

"There are some things that should never be said. 'If something does not go according to your plans or your liking, and you get angry and complain,' and you say 'I should most certainly die and so should you,' or say something like 'the sky and land should both collapse,' or 'make the house and the nation fall into ruin,' or say to the other, 'drift about and beg,' then all these phrases and similar ones should not be said, as they are ominous and rude.

"There are some things that should never be heard, and 'dirty talk, or talk beyond one's station, or vain talk, or talking badly about someone, or lying, or harsh words, or exaggerated talk, or cold words due to wanting to avenge something,' should be avoided at all costs and you should never respond to such talk."

"If during a conversation, 'If I hear from someone else something contrary to what I have heard, then I should not keep on insisting that I am right and break the spirit of the other person, and I should avoid speaking at length about it.'"

"And say things discreetly, for 'things that I hear without proof, or words on the street, or vague words, or words that may be true,' must not be repeated to another in a friendly manner."

Is this not an excellent teaching?

Lastly, there are manners between young people that are not used well today, and that is called "apjonbeop," or using the honorifics in reverse. This refers to when a person addresses someone as his superior and uses honorifics that pertain to the person he is talking to, whilst not using the most formal of the tenses when referring to someone who is even more higher-ranking. I see this mistake often.

For example, saying "Grandpa, Father is coming," and using the tense, "oshimnida," is wrong. The correct wording is "Grandpa, Father is coming," and using the tense, "opnida."

Manners Regarding One's Superiors and Teachers/Mentors

Let me quote again from the *Sohak* and *Sasojeol.*

In the *Gokrye* is a saying, "If a person is more than twice your age, then treat him as you would your father, and for a person who is about ten years older, treat him as an older brother, and for a person who is five years ahead of you, walk with your shoulders straight but trail him a little bit." "Those who are hosts of a gentleman should take care not to answer a question he poses without glancing around the room first, for this does not denote manners."

Additionally, in *Liji* there are teachings regarding how to receive and host one's elders.

"If the elder person is about the same age as your father, then do not ask him his age, and when visiting in private, do not have a servant send a message but instead, enter the room yourself and pay your respects, and when you encounter him on the street in a serendipitous occasion, if the elder is on his way home, go visit him soon, rather than asking where he is going."

"When you are hosting the elder, if the elder did not direct you, then do not take a musical instrument into your hands, and do not draw on the ground, and gesticulate, or fan a fan. When the elder is lying down, if there is a message to be conveyed, then please have him sit up then relay it, and do not relay it while standing up and gazing down at him."

In the *Sohak*, when you are accompanying an elder and traveling, "if the elder is about the age of your father, then follow him from behind, and if he is about your older brother's age, then you may swagger a little but trail behind him a bit, and if he is of the same age, then walk shoulder to shoulder with him. Hold a light load by yourself, but a larger one, share, and do not let a man who is half a century old carry heavy loads by himself."

When you are receiving guests and sending them off, the *Sasojeol* says, "If you are sending off a guest who is about knee high, then please follow him to the end of the floor, and when the guest is your age, then clasp his hands and rise from your seat, then see him off until he steps down from the ledge, then sit down again. If the guest has barely risen from his seat and has not yet left via the front door, do not sit down again hastily, for you may still be visible and this is a pompous thing to do."

"When with another person, do not lean on the wall with your legs stretched out, for speaking while lying down is crude behavior."

"When an elder asks about your age, you must say twenty or thirty as an estimate, for you must not refer to the twelve-year cycle of the Chinese zodiac. This is because of the possibility that the elder will not be able to quickly calculate your age."

"This is a thoughtful admonition."

For Koreans, it is customary that even a high-ranking government official should not be treated so highly in the home. As I have stated before, while quoting from the *Gokrye*, even a person of distinction fails to rank higher than a guest.

Koreans may be familiar with the story of Yulgok, who taught that the middle brother, who was clumsy at everything, always beckoned to him every time he had to finish a task. Yulgok did his bidding every single time, while not frowning nor was he ever lazy.

This behavior so irked his servants, for he was a high-ranking official in government, that one of them asked him, "How can you do the work in his stead for is this not too respectful?" Yulgok replied, "Father orders me to do something, so how could I disregard his order? For in front of his father, there should only be a deep sense of respect."

"This is also not by coincidence, and a government official in this instance should not debate whether this is a low or high thing to do," he said.

Lastly, I will relay some more wisdom from *Gokrye*, regarding how to treat one's teachers.

"When you are receiving your teacher as a guest and when he asks you something, you must respond after he has finished speaking. When you ask him to teach lessons, you must be standing. When you are listening to his lecture, you must be standing."

More of the same, below:

"For in the future, when returning to your seat, you must not be shy or disoriented, but you must fold both hands together and rise from the floor and back away. Your clothes must not flutter and your feet, not move in haste."

"If the teacher's book or his musical instrument, or mandolin, is in the way, you must place them to the side gently, without stepping over them."

"When you are sitting, you must sit up straight, and your complexion should be clear."

"If an elder has not finished speaking you must not interject with your words regarding some other matters, for he may become perplexed."

"When the teacher gives a lecture, you must have a good glow to your face, and listen carefully and respectfully, and not claim someone else's theory for your own, nor agree with someone else's claims without careful consideration. You must consider the old wisdom of the ancients as law, and the wisdom of the late king should be considered when writing or during discussion."

My dears, this may have been boring for you.

I would like to interject with an anecdote from the Meiji Restoration period in Japan.

Formerly a country composed of feudal states, in the nineteenth century, Japan underwent a transformation and became a modern state.

They sent some of their best and brightest abroad to learn from the West, especially with regard to its culture. Those samurai who were chosen to go abroad to study stepped on books that had been imported from the West, in homage to their native Japanese culture; it was a symbolic gesture, meant to demonstrate that they would stay loyal to Japan and return as Japanese.

Some may see this as narrow-minded, but I think otherwise.

Perhaps the politicians of the day worried that Western ideology and customs would take precedence over their native Japanese culture, so it was really in keeping with what they wished for Japan in the future; the preservation of it and its culture. In essence, Grandpa believes it was a wise decision.

Japan today, as you are very well aware, is now a developed nation that stands shoulder to shoulder with Germany and France in terms of its economic prowess and is also a wealthy country, like the United States of America. China may have surpassed it in terms of wealth, recently, I believe. But even as a developed country, it has managed to preserve its unique Eastern culture, steeped in tradition. Japan is a modern country, thanks to its leaders during the nineteenth century, and these forebearers were wise and their discernment, somewhat astonishing.

The reason why Grandpa wanted to teach you the lessons from the past, even if they may have been boring to you, is because you need to know our cultural roots. That does not mean that one has to keep these roots verbatim all the time. You must know the roots, add to them from other cultures, perhaps, and make them stronger.

One thing to guard against as you do this, is the fallacy in believing you are always right, and, ironically, that you are always wrong, and abandon everything and copy the other, which you regard superior to your own.

"Manners are a form of affection," as Grandpa's mentor once put, and as he said, do not sway to either side but keep loyal to the roots and do not lose the fundamentals...do you see what I mean?

Chapter 9

Home Economics

Neither Too Much nor Too Little

On Money

Learn How to Fish First

Neither Too Much nor Too Little

A boat becomes lost at sea due to a strong squall. A wave as large as a mountain threatens to capsize the boat. At any moment, it may swallow it up. Nightmares and daymares bleed into days.

The storm suddenly stops one day, and the sun shines brightly. You can see the island, far off in the distance. The captain and the sailors on board shout, "We're safe!" and celebrate. The island beckons with promises of trees and flowers in full bloom and the warm scent of flowers and ripe fruit beckons to them.

At this moment, the people on board suddenly divide into three groups.

The first group says, "Let us not disembark. We do not know when a fair wind may come to us. For our safety, let us stay on the boat." This group looks at the bounty of Nature the island seems to offer, but chooses to stay onboard the stuffy boat. They wait in silence for the fair wind.

The second group says, "Let us disembark and at least whet our thirst by the springs on the island." They do so, take in the beautiful flowers, and eat the delicious fruit. And return on board when the boat starts its preparations to leave.

The third group disembarks and enjoys the bounty of Nature for days. They go further inland, drawn by the strange and delicious fruit, unaware that the boat has already left.

For every person, there is something called your "lot." The elders of old knew the fate of each man, and everyone was encouraged to keep it and not exceed it. But this is no easy task.

The reason why it's difficult to stay within budget is because of human greed. They squander their fortune to dine well and wear expensive designer clothing…and honor and power can sometimes be begotten from money. If greed didn't exist, then I am of the opinion that man could not have lived and thrived on this Earth. For greed feeds intrinsic motivation sometimes. But at the same time, because of greed we need to keep a balanced checkbook, and because of this greed, it is difficult to stay within one's budget.

Like many things, both extremes exist. There is long and short, bravery and cowardice, and rich and poor. You cannot use it because it is too long, and you are too brave, you may be foolhardy, and if your bank account is overflowing, you also have trouble spending money. Along the same lines, even if it is too short, you cannot use it, and if you are cowardly, you cannot be of use, and you cannot spend money if you are too poor.

"You can choose to get drunk or stay sober, but getting drunk affects one's integrity, and you can choose to give or not give, but if you choose to not give then it will damage your friendship, and you can choose to die or not but dying is cowardly and damages bravery." So says Mencius.

That is why the sages of old taught the path of moderation. It must not overflow but not be too meager…it is choosing the middle way, to be fair. Is moderation not another word for knowing one's lot?

This is referred to as "joongyong." Confucius uses an example to demonstrate the path of moderation.

Boyi and Yiyin differed in their ways of living.• Boyi refused to serve unless it was under his own king, and refused to help the citizens if they were not from his region, and when the nation was peaceful he served in a government post and during times of turmoil he withdrew from government duties. Yiyin, on the other hand, said cryptically, "Are not anyone you serve Kings, and anyone who helps the citizens, one's own countrymen?" He served in government during times of peace and during times of turmoil.

But Confucius says to go out in the world to serve as a government official if you can, and resign when you must, and if you can serve in that post for a long time, do so, and if you cannot, leave quickly.

Mencius names all three, but the only enlightened one is Confucius, he says. Boyi is not one for the ages because he is too inflexible and Yiyin he admires for his innocence but finds fault in his lack of humility. But Confucius knows the right timing, of when to leave and when to stay, and thus follows the "joongyong," or the path of moderation. Mencius regards him as the true master.

You must eat in accordance with your lot, spend money in accordance with one's lot, and exercise power and authority in accordance with one's lot. This is the way of living a life of reason. This will prevent your world from becoming topsy-turvy.

The ones who got drunk on the scent of the flowers and the fruit, and failed to see the boat leave, are the ones who do not know reason. The ones who stayed aboard the stuffy boat and waited for a fair wind are also those who do not know reason.

• Boyi was from the Shang Dynasty and was the son of Gohjukgun. He was also the older brother of Sukje. After bidding goodbye to King Wu of Zhou, he entered Suyangsan Mountain and lived by digging up some ferns. Yiyin also hailed from the Shang Dynasty and was a well-known statesman and served King Tang.

On Money

Money is a strange thing. It has two faces, like the Greek god Janus. Francis Bacon once said of money, "Money is a great servant but a bad master." Depending on how it is used, money can become your master or your servant.

There are others who may say, "Money is at the root of all evil, and the source of all grief and agony." However, there are those like Goethe, who says, "A heavy purse makes the heart lighter." There is another British adage that says, "If you knock on a door with money, there are no doors you cannot open."

There is another Western proverb worth mentioning here: "When I had a lot of money, I had many servants, and when I had money, people called me brother." But another proverb, also from the West, says, "I have lost more friends than gained them due to money." Now do you see that money, and how it is used, and one's opinion of it, changes from person to person? A simpleton may become confused by money.

But children, I have said it once and I will say it again, that money is a good thing. It's an important thing. It's also very valuable. Without money, you cannot eat right now, nor clothe yourself. If you are so poor you cannot afford food, then where will you find dignity or honor? That is why you shouldn't ignore money and you should not appear vulgar and you must not reject money either.

John Wesley, the founder of the Methodist church, once said of money, "Earn money…as much as you can. Save money…as much as you can. And give as much as you can." Even a poor but honest man like Wesley said this.

The problem is that one should not be debating whether money is good or not, but ponder how to use it properly.

There is a Russian proverb: "Fertilizer that has been saved for later has a bad smell, while the fertilizer that has been spread on the earth makes the land fertile." Like fertilizer, money is for the using. You cannot save it for just yourself. Rather, you should use it for others as well. Then like the earth becoming fertile, society will become brighter and the worth of money will shine brighter still.

People sometimes borrow things and let others borrow things too. You can borrow books, and cars, and even homes, these days. But when borrowing money, there are some things worth considering.

A Western proverb says, "If you want to make an enemy of your friend, lend him money."

Why? "If you lend money, then you will lose both the money and your friend," says the *Talmud*. The same is said in *Hamlet*, "Neither a borrower nor a lender be; For loan oft loses both itself and friend."

That is why it is wise to not borrow or lend money. If you cannot escape lending money for some reason, then as circumstances permit, it is better just to give it away.

"Wealth is a fortress, and poverty is ruin," says the *Talmud*. You must have enough money at all times in order not to be a burden on another person. Then you must earn money, as much and as hard as you can. I am referring to hard work and sweat here. You must also earn money in an honest way. Then you will be able to make your home a fortress.

Learn How to Fish First

The first thing to teach a child is that a person's salary should be proportional to his efforts. Money requires hard work and sweat. That is when the child will learn that money is precious. A child should also learn about money's uses and power. You should also teach them about how money can also be dangerous and cause harm.

When you are young, it is not easy to know about money. That is why money doesn't just appear out of the blue. It should follow hard work. Running errands, doing good, mowing grass…the list goes on. Give them money after these tasks if the child is working hard. This should become a habit.

Sometimes I have seen Westerners look down on us because we waste money and we are not punctual about settling our accounts. Sometimes I may be privy to this too (the latter). I did not really know the ins and outs of money, and no one ever taught me about the characteristics of money either.

In our long history, you know that "We should treat a gold like a stone." This metaphor means that you should not be blinded by wealth. Between upper class folk, money transfers, and the like, or even talking about money was frowned upon.

Most people thought of money in terms of an allowance given to children during the Lunar New Year, and it was thought crude to think about money.

But times have changed. I need not explain this further.

The Westerners say, "A foolish man cannot master money."

You must control money, however, for do you want to suffer the burden of loans crushing your back?

The next step is to give children an allowance. An allowance should not be too much, but just the right amount that they can spend. If you give them too little money, they will not be able to keep up with their peers and will develop jealous qualities and bad habits.

If there is something a child wants, then if it is not too excessive, it is best to give it to him. You should give it as a reward for hard work. You can give it to him on special occasions, like birthdays, but the more he wants it the more you have to make him "earn" it.

The Jewish people, from what I know, teach children to buy things for themselves, so that they learn the importance of keeping within budget. No wonder why the financial world is run by the Jewish people.

If you give a child an allowance, then you must also follow up on how he spends it. Have him keep a tally of his expenditures and at the end of every month, parents should examine it.

In Korean culture, there is a saying, "A child who will make his ancestors proud will treat even fertilizer like gold, while a child who will bring ruin to his family will spend money like trash."

In the *Talmud*, it says, "Instead of giving them fish, teach them how to fish."

In the East, there is a man named Taegong, who says, "Meager skill will win over a good field," so we should teach them skills as well.

Money is not golden, nor is it stone.

There are things that cannot be bought with money. Money may sometimes paralyze peoples' morality, but cannot change character. You may act in self-interest at first, but your character will predict how you will spend the money.

You may be able to buy honor with money, but not friends or loyalty with it.

Chapter 10

Let's Live a Happy Life

First and Foremost Is Health

In our family, we have a saying, "Eating gives you strength." We exchange this saying between ourselves. This may even be our family motto. I'm not joking, for taking this as a family motto may be an excellent thing for us to do. If the family motto is working hard and diligence, it may be too ideological, so that is why I prefer the other phrase.

I always say this, but actions speak louder than words. An adage that is vague is not a good one, because you cannot put it into action. A person who dines well and sleeps well is a healthy person. You must also eat well and sleep well in order to regain your health.

Health is the first requirement of living a happy life, and is being healthy not a requirement for many things?

No matter how wealthy you are, if you are unhealthy, you will never feel happy. No matter how brilliant you are, if you are unhealthy, then life will not be pleasurable. If you want to become healthy, then you must eat well. Dining should be pleasurable. When you wake up in the morning you will be full of energy and will never know tiredness, even if you are running from one place to another. If you have the means to dine well, then this alone can also be defined as happiness.

If at first gastronomy delights you, then the second is to learn new things and exchange ideas and form a friendship with a wise person.

What do I mean by this? If you dine with someone who is in a different line of work, then you will learn new things and also gain a good friend. From people we meet all the time it is hard to earn this kind of opportunity. You must keep on meeting new people, and as circumstances and your wallet permits, dine with them.

The famous German philosopher, Immanuel Kant,• is known for his enjoyment of taking long walks and encouraging others to do so as well, but it's not well known that he used to take long lunches. The average lunch for him would take three hours, and sometimes he would take six hours. Do you think he was wasting time?

No, of course not. It's because the time is spent less on eating than on conversation.

Kant was a famous philosopher and was also an excellent conversationalist. With many prominent persons of the day, he would be invited as a guest, and he would also sit in company with them and sometimes these lunches would turn into debates. Kant added to his knowledge by doing this, but this method of dining also helped him work in the intellectual circles he was accustomed to moving in.

Third, the happiness of dining well is that you can befriend new people and also deepen friendships. There are few ways of making lasting friendships and building relationships with people other than dining with them. If you dine well, then you will become healthier, and when you dine well, you will be happier, so do you now see that "Eating gives you strength." is not a mere joke?

There are those who spend sleepless nights. They suffer from insomnia. It is indicative of a disease.

• Immanuel Kant (1724–1804) was a German philosopher who may be known as the father of modern philosophy. His works include the *Critique of Pure Reason*, the *Critique of Practical Reason*, and the *Critique of Judgment*.

A person who doesn't sleep well cannot live a happy life. A person deprived of sleep must at least get to the root of the problems keeping him up at night.

If a person has no worries and is still unable to sleep, then this becomes a problem. But it's not a difficult disease to resolve. If you are physically tired, you are apt to become sleepy. Why not walk 10,000 steps a day, or play tennis for an hour, or swim for thirty minutes—there are many ways to tire yourself out.

If these tactics don't work, then increase the time you exercise. Before sleeping, drink a glass of warm milk. When you are older, a glass of white wine is a good remedy for those sleepless nights.

The reason why a warm glass of milk is conducive to sleep is because it harkens back to childhood, and our early days as an infant.

Too many times, I have seen doctors prescribe medication, but this is the worst course of action to take. If exercise and warm milk don't do the trick, don't take medications; rather, increase your physical activity. Remember, avoid sleeping pills at all costs.

You should try to gather your thoughts at night, in bed, and recite from the Bible. My favorite one is, "He maketh me to lie down in green pastures: He leadeth me beside the still waters" (Psalms 23:2).

If this doesn't work, then try self-hypnosis. Take a deep breath, then say, "I am falling into a deep sleep," three times. When you are reciting this loud, focus on your inner self and whisper.

If you do this, then your inner self will accept, generously, that you need to sleep. The deep breathing techniques I have mentioned in a previous chapter will help you.

Now let us turn to work and play. All work and no play make Jack a dull boy. It's bad to just work, and it's bad to just play. You must work hard and play hard because this is the key to an enjoyable and happy life. That is why you must know how to play.

Ants are some of the hardest-working creatures on this Earth.

According to entomologists, it may appear that ants do nothing but work busily all day long, but they also play.

They may poke the Queen Ant with their heads, and upon leaving their colony, may look at strange and mysterious (to them) items. The topography of the land may make them examine it by going around it in circles. Sometimes, they may gaze vacantly at something far away.

The sad part is, however, that an ant that doesn't engage in play has no flexibility for when hard times strike.

When scientists took ants who played all day with ants who worked all day, and split them into groups and released them somewhat at a distance from the ant colony, the ants that had played had no problems finding their way home, but those who had no chance to play were unable to find their way home, for they got lost.

When you play, play hard. When you play, you will be happy, and people who play well also work well, so why the hesitation? Let's play. Play hard.

Hobbies and Favorite Items

Hobbies and favorite items enrich our lives, from day to day. Hobbies can be as varied and versatile as you wish. You can pick them based on your economic situation and your personality.

There is a Western adage that says, "A fool wanders about, but a sensible person goes on vacation." As time and your budget allow, go on a trip, and if you are feeling down, go on a hike. You should choose where you hike based on the season.

Pink azaleas may greet you during the spring, and in the fall, the leaves will be ablaze with various colors, and during the winter, Mount Seorak will also be good for viewing the snow. If you'd like, you can take photographs with a camera, and or paint. Is there a better photographer and or painter than you? I think not. Who cares if you are an amateur?

Collecting things can also be a hobby. Collect books, rare money, stamps, rocks, and the like. There really is no end to collecting things.

Taking up exercise as a hobby is "ilseokijo," or killing two birds with one stone. Swimming is a great way to exercise, and is playing a round or two of tennis not enjoyable?

You can also watch plays and movies, and even act in a small group of amateur actors and grace the stage. You can even play some songs that you've heard on the radio on a musical instrument if you take a hobby that far.

Becoming an artist, a photographer, an athlete, an actor in plays, and a musician…the world is your oyster. Who cares if you are an amateur?

It's been over thirty years (as of this first printing) since I left the Korean Army. If I did not have a guitar during this time, I could not have borne that difficult time period without even more difficulty. Grandma and I learned together and played music that was popular during that time and sang as well. On teary days and nights, I felt as though playing the guitar acted like a salve to both our wounds.

There is a Japanese saying, "A bad hobby is better than no hobby at all." Well, there is no real reason why you should take up a bad hobby, but having a hobby is really important in life and takes up a lot of space, is what it's really conveying.

As far as favorite items go, it may really boil down to cigarettes and alcohol. These days, it's like a sin to smoke in public. That's how much it's frowned upon. Smokers have nowhere to go, it seems, for most places are now non-smoking. On the airplane, in restaurants, in public areas…there are no more places that welcome smokers.

I, for my part, stopped smoking over thirty years ago. For my health. My little angels, I frown upon smoking for ladies. For the men of our family, I do not recommend they smoke. I recommend not smoking, instead.

Cigarettes are not good for your health, that much is clear. However, they act like a stimulants, and I've heard that they may stop neurosis (nonsmokers were apt to suffer more frequently from neurosis). This is what the smokers say, anyway.

However, cigarettes are cancerous, for smoking raises the risk of certain cancers, for example. But as I've said before, I am not going to forbid smoking for the men of our family.

Someone I regard as a hero of World War II, Great Britain's Prime Minister Winston Churchill, once had an audience with Major General Bernard Montgomery. It was entirely due to chance.

When Churchill praised Montgomery for his health, he said, "Sir, I have never touched a drop of liquor or held a cigarette to my lips. That is my recipe for good health." He obliquely was praising his nonsmoking, no-alcohol lifestyle.

Churchill, who was rarely seen without a cigar in his mouth and was a great lover of the drink as well, then supposedly replied, "General, I have never been without a cigar in my mouth, and whiskey is my friend, for I drink it every day. But I am still so healthy that I am in the Head Office at Downing Street."

Montgomery was one of the greatest generals in history. His British forces quelled German forces in North Africa, specifically, at the Battle of El-Alamein. The Germans were led by General Erwin Rommel. This was during World War II.

He is comparable to the great General Wellington who dashed the hopes of Napoleon at the Battle of Waterloo, years before on European soil.

For a General, abstaining from drinking, and not smoking may be good habits to instill, but then again, Churchill's love for smoking and bacchanal ways are not that bad, in my opinion.

These days, more research has revealed that smoking is bad not just for the person who is smoking, but for others as well. Second-hand smoke is also detrimental to health, so when you are around others, keep this in mind and don't smoke.

As I have said before, the women of this family are forbidden from smoking.

"The pipe draws wisdom from the philosopher, and closes the mouth of the foolish," says William M. Thackeray.• Perhaps that is why Immanuel Kant's breakfast consisted of just two cups of tea and a cigarette.

French playwright Moliere,•• once said, "There is no reason for living without being able to smoke."

But there is another saying in the West, which says, "The unfortunate smoke, and the more you smoke, the more dire your circumstances become."

• William M. Thackeray (1811–1863), was one of the fathers of British "Realism." He was well-regarded as a novelist and artist for his humor and wit. His most famous work is the novel *Vanity Fair.*

•• Moliere (1622–1673) was a French playwright known for his comedies written for the stage. Many of his characters displayed complexity and exposed what he regarded as the lies of society. *Tartuffe* and *Le Misanthrope* are two of his most famous plays.

If you, as a member of this family, must smoke, then keep this in mind: "Do not harm others with your smoking."

As an aside, Grandpa has a pipe worth half a million U.S. dollars. Don't be astounded. The pipe did not cost half a million but it's worth that much. So how did this come about?

In the 1970's, I was in the Middle East for work. The first place I traveled to was Qatar. The national land mass is about 11,490 km squared. The capital is Doha.

It is now a semi-constitutional monarchy, and as far as I know, it was the first out of all the Middle Eastern countries to commission the building of an iron factory. They were good at making money.

I remember that when getting into a vehicle, the wealthy would sit shotgun next to the driver, while his bodyguards sat in the back.

While the company I worked for was building the iron factory, a wealthy man asked us to construct a building. About a month's worth of negotiations later, we were given the green light to proceed, with the signing and the stamping of the contract to be done after lunch.

After lunch, we convened. As you know, it's hot in the Middle East, and Qatar was no exception. Lunches, from what I remember, used to take several hours because lunch would be followed by a siesta. That is why lunch hours were from about noon to 3:00 or 4:00 p.m.

But what was this! We had agreed in the morning to facilitate the operations in the afternoon, but his attitude had completely changed. He actually had the audacity to ask for a price cut of 500,000 U.S. dollars. I understood his reasoning, but still, I thought the wealthy man was shameless. So I closed my lips and took out the pipe that I had with me. I then took out the tobacco pouch, filled the pipe's bowl, then quietly lit it.

I did this leisurely.

For cigarettes, it usually takes about three minutes to smoke per cigarette. For pipes, it averages around twenty minutes, normally, and you can extend the time sometimes. There is an art to smoking a pipe. To this day, there is even an international championship (the CIPC Pipe Slow Smoking World Championships) to prove it.

I decided to vacantly stare at the other man, whilst smoking the pipe. During that time, I had to light it twice, so over twenty minutes must have passed. The tobacco started tasting bitter in my mouth, so it must have been actually over thirty minutes. At this time, the wealthy man leaped up from his seat, and said, "Fine, have it your way!"

The man's name, I recall, was Al-obeldi. The building was twenty-two stories high, and for a country where buildings over four stories high were non-existent (in the capital of Qatar, anyway), it was practically a monument. When I visited five years ago, there were so many buildings over fifty floors high. There must have been at least a hundred of them.

With the exception of lovers, it is rare to have two people gaze at each other without talking for over three minutes. But thanks to the pipe, the silence was bearable, for about thirty minutes, at least; and that was all that I had needed.

I still have the $500,000 pipe in my possession. I am an impatient man, so I owe the pipe even more thanks.

The pipe tests the average person's patience, and for the person without patience, makes him empty his pockets.

Is Alcohol the Instrument of the Devil?

Out of all human possessions, alcohol is enchanting but dangerous. Other than the creation of alcoholics, there are many societal problems caused by drinking that need to be addressed.

It is said that Bacchus, the god of wine, drowned more men than the god Neptune, who ruled the oceans.

But I do not agree with pundits who say that alcohol should be banned. There are some Islamic countries in the Middle East, where alcohol is never served. However, I am of the opinion that when a country outlaws alcohol, other crimes and societal problems become bigger. I would like to mention Chicago's gangs and crime during the Prohibition era in the United States of America (this is where Al Capone made his name and fortune as a member of the Mafia).

The history of alcohol must date back centuries, to when civilization started. Greek and Roman mythology mentions wine and even our East Asian ancestors' myths address drink.

According to *The History of the Three Kingdoms*, the founder of Goguryeo, Jumong, was conceived through drink. It says that the son of Cheonje (Heaven), Haemosu, got the three daughters of Habaek (a tribal head) drunk, prevented them from returning to the palace, then took the eldest of the three, Yuhwa, as his wife.

Alcohol has been long used for putting women at risk, so be prudent.

In Greek and Roman mythology, the god of wine is Bacchus (Dionysius). But Bacchus' birth is a tragedy in and of itself. He was born to a human woman, Semele, and the god Zeus. Zeus' wife, Hera, who was jealous of Semele, made Zeus burn the other woman to death. Zeus managed to rescue his son, who barely managed to see the light of day.

Bacchus, born from fire and ashes, made the grapes ripe under the hot sun, and made the plants grow when it rained. When he reached adulthood, he went to different regions and taught them how to cultivate grapes. This is how wine originated and how wine spread to different parts of the world.

In the *Talmud*, there is a different anecdote about the origins of wine.

The first man was cultivating grapes in a vineyard when he received an unexpected visitor. The Devil came to visit him, bringing with him a lamb, a lion, a pig, and a monkey. The Devil requested a portion of the grapes for himself. When the first man agreed to it, the Devil killed the four animals and poured the blood on the ground, to be used as fertilizer for the fruit. This is how the grapes grew ripe and wine flowed like blood.

Afterward, whenever drinking, at first, you are like a sweet lamb, and when you drink a little more, you turn into a cantankerous lion, and when you drink a little bit more, you become as slovenly as a pig, then finally, at the last sip, you become a monkey that dances and sings. That is why alcohol is a gift from the Devil, or so they say.

Well, isn't this true? There is a lot of talk about wine and lots of accidents, besides. That is why you must keep a level head whilst drinking.

The first rule when drinking is knowing moderation.

Just as you need to moderate your actions, you need to moderate your intake of wine. First, you must know how much to drink, and how to behave with the person you are drinking with, and third, where to go to drink with your partner, and fourth, know which types of wine to drink, and fifth, how to look whilst drinking. That is why the consumption of wine is an art.

There is an art to drinking wine, and if you complain about having to think so much whilst drinking, then you don't have any right to drink.

You drink when you are happy, you drink when you are sad, and drink it because you wish to, and drink because you're angry, and sometimes, you drink because you are forced to. That is why you must practice moderation, you must at least think about the rules behind the art of drinking at least once, before imbibing.

Long ago, when the world was created for man, remember that if you are not careful, you become a lion, then a pig, then a monkey. This is a warning to the male members of the family.

They talk a lot about the etiquette behind drinking wine, and Grandpa has wondered about this, but have reached the conclusion that there really isn't any.

Once, I met with my venerable mentor and asked him, "Could you tell me more about the ancient ceremony of wine drinking?" For a long time, he did not say anything, then he brought up another topic of conversation. I wondered if I was not up to the task yet of becoming his student, so I refrained from peppering him with more questions.

It was customary for him, an elder, to not answer if he was displeased with his guest, so I believe I don't have any right to debate over this question and refrained from asking him anymore.

One day, the venerable Weoltan[•] told me about a banquet that he had attended a long time ago.

• Park Jong-hwa (1901–1981), also known as Weoltan, was a Korean poet, novelist, and professor. His works include historical fiction written in the Korean, such as *Geum-sam's Blood*, *Don't Trust Dae-Jung*, and *The Dragon's Invasion*.

"I would invite guests and bring the liquor, but only place one drinking glass on the table. After I drank first, as the host, then every guest would drink from the same cup. This is called 'soonbae' (passing the glass one after another at a drinking party). That is why the spirit is moderated and there is no chance of drinking too much."

He said this matter-of-factly and in his very still eyes, I could sense a longing for his teacher who had taught him this, but at the same time, was his longing to drink more of the delicious beverage.

"So passing one cup around is customary for us Koreans?"

"Young man. What do you mean by rule? I told you, 'etiquette is affection.'"

He must have become annoyed by my eagerness to know more, but I was even more annoyed.

He was a man of few words, to begin with, and he refrained from more explanations; an ordinary person like me could not win over him.

When a child reaches seventh grade (year one of middle school in Korea), a father should choose a day to drink with him. The father will teach the growing boy how to pour and drink alcohol. The effects of alcohol and what I have mentioned in the previous pages about moderation regarding alcohol are the two things that must be conveyed to the boy at this time.

It's not too fast for the boy if he enters middle school. Once a child reaches middle school, it's not uncommon for them to start drinking out of curiosity amongst themselves. That is why it is preferable to teach them before they start drinking with friends. Drink together, let him taste the alcohol, and let him experience first-hand the changes to his body and mind after drinking.

What a somber and monumental occasion, to drink before one's father. How insightful would this education be?

Myself included, there are many in this world who make mistakes that they regret upon drinking.

If in China, you get drunk and start making a scene, then you become an outcast of society. In the United States, a similar move will cost the person a public office. East and West, I encourage moderation in drinking. There are those who cannot win over alcohol, and these people are also bad at working. You cannot trust them with a big task either. Is there not an adage in the West regarding drinking, about how it loosens one's lips to reveal secrets?

What if circumstances led you to drink in excess? The first thing to do is stop and go home. If you cannot, lie down in the next room or on the floor. It's better to be condemned than to make a mistake after getting drunk.

Alas, I may have said too many things to turn your taste for alcohol.

But alcohol in and of itself is actually (I may be contradicting myself here) a good thing. The only thing to guard against is that some drink in excess or in the wrong way, which damages not just a person but his reputation and his health as well.

What types of alcohol do I recommend? They are all good. Alcohol made from fermented grains, alcohol made from fruit, hard liquor, all are preferable. Beer and wine, especially, are also deeply ingrained in our culinary culture these days.

Makgeolli (rice wine), soju (hard liquor), whiskey…let us talk about these later.

Some people are scared of wine, for it may require specialized knowledge. But it's like all others; made for drinking. There is no need to be particular. If you have a little bit of knowledge about wine then you can drink it as well as a Westerner. There are many good books on wine.

Wine has a long history and is nothing short of miraculous. All alcohol is acidic with the exception of wine, which is alkaline. Among its other qualities, a unique trait is that it helps with thinking and encourages your brain to remain active.

Yes, there have been studies that say alcohol damages the brain, yet people who are intellectual and very successful seem to have all drank wine. There are records of this.

Goethe used to drink two bottles of white wine produced in Germany per day. Kant forwent dinner but always had a large lunch accompanied by French wine. Both remained active intellectually, even in their later years.

Beer, on the other hand, has an effect on the human body that is different from wine; some might say the opposite effect. The British do not really get excited, some say, because they have drunk beer for centuries. Beer makes a person more pliable, shall we say. That is why when you need to nurse your own wounds (metaphorically speaking), drink beer instead of wine.

You must always guard against drinking too much. Is there not a Western proverb that says that when the Devil is too busy to visit in person, he sends alcohol instead?

An Intellectual Life

Knowledge is happiness itself and is a delight. When you learn one thing, it exceeds the happiness that you feel after eating, and one realization can lead to our hearts becoming fuller. It's like quenching thirst, but better. That is why intellectual activities in and of themselves are enjoyable.

Happiness is not far away. There are treasure boxes waiting to be opened. They are bookshelves full of books or your study.

Keep books close by. Unlike alcohol or money, there are no bad books and no bad effects from devouring them. It does not make demands, nor does it burden you. A book is a hardworking friend and or an excellent teacher.

Unfortunately, there are too many good books to read, and you will be unable to read all of the ones you have picked out. If they are classics, so much the better. I do think that not all books are worth reading, so take heed.

It's best to speed-read, for there are so many books to read. You can read two lines at a time. When you are trained in this, it will not be uncomfortable. Underline a good passage or sentence, and write notes in the margins.

There are good books, and books that you personally find delightful. Then you should read these books carefully. If need be, read more than once. A good book must be read several times, because every time you read it, you will reach new, deeper revelations and the feeling won't be the same.

Read in bright light. Otherwise, you will harm your vision. The reason why my vision worsened is because when I was a second lieutenant in the Korean Army, I read in the cold of winter under a dim kerosene lamp. I was stationed in Gangwon Province then.

When able, regularly visit bookstores, for they will bring you joy. Isn't it great to be surrounded by mountains of books? And if you are lucky, you will buy and leave with a good book.

You can also visit church bookstores or even little shops in the countryside that sell books. The latter, unlike book chains, you may find some forgotten treasures. There are many books that are no longer in print, and you may find some there. Big bookstore chains usually push contemporary or new books, and because they are so large, may be unwieldy.

The Pursuit of Beauty

In the *Sohak*, the section called, "Entering Education," talks about how once you reach the age of thirteen, a person should "learn music and read and memorize poetry and learn dance."

"From the age of fifteen, he should learn rougher dances and learn how to shoot an arrow and ride a horse," so says the book.

Confucius once asked his son, named Li, who was passing by a garden, "Have you learned poetry?" The son replied in the negative.

Then Confucius supposedly said, "If you did not learn poetry, then there must be no topics of conversation that you can broach."

All these are teachings from 2,000 years ago. Even back then, our ancestors stressed the importance of singing and dancing. Confucius's greatness is surprising.

There are too many beautiful things in this world. One of the sources of great happiness in this lifetime is the pursuit of beauty.

The sunrise, the twinkling stars at night, the flowers that bloom to the beautiful fall foliage, Hyo Sung and Hae-Yeon...

If you pass by a morning glory that has grown alone, you will see it wilt by itself by nightfall. No matter how warm the morning sunshine, if you do not bless God in all His glory you are sure to meet death sooner rather than later.

The beauty of autumn and the colorful leaves are beautiful because I exist. This is because I sing for the beauty of the fall foliage. If humans did not exist on this green Earth, then I hesitate to say that this beautiful Earth may be just another planet, circling the sun in a void, for there are no humans to appreciate its beauty.

"Beauty is truth," as defined by the English poet John Keats.

I will now recount an anecdote from when I was in Jinhae, as an officer student at Army College.

I missed home, Daegu, a three-hour drive from Jinhae, and decided on a whim to go home. I wasn't actually going home to visit anyone in particular. It wasn't if I had urgent business to attend to, either. I just decided to go on a whim.

I rode a combination of taxis and buses and viewed the quiet suburbs for hours out the window.

The mountains were so beautiful. It wasn't just because it was in autumn, where the trees are cloaked in autumnal foliage. Gangwon Province is noted for its beautiful fall foliage, and I'd had my fill of it when I had been stationed there, my eyes going red from viewing too long the majestic reds, golds, oranges, and yellows....

With golden fields outside my window, going from high to low (Korea is a mountainous country), interspersed with the mountains and other fields, with the blue skies high above...how did this beautiful vista play off of each other in perfect harmony?

Since the taxi was racing ahead I too was in transit, with the golden fields and hills giving in suddenly to rivers, then mountains growing larger and larger as I traversed close to them.

I say that even small mountains' autumn leaves are so beautiful as well.

If you were to say fall leaves, I would have said Naejangsan Mountain, and if you had talked to me of a snowy landscape, I would have immediately said Seorak Mountain. I had always viewed the two as disparate from one another; fall foliage in one region and a snowy mountain in another.

After that day, however, I realized that beauty could be found in commonplace areas, in ordinary brooks of all places, and small, what you might say, ordinary mountains. Viewing these places gave me more pleasure than the well-known ones.

If you refer to great mountains, would you have mentioned perhaps Gangwon Province's steep peaks or even the greater Himalayan peaks? I hope not. Gangwon Province's peaks are beautiful and native to the area. The peaks of the Himalayas give off a brilliant and magnificent sight.

However, there is beauty to be found in a common plain that can only be found in such places. No one place is superior to another. What I found beautiful or ugly are my personal preferences for talking, and not the mountain's fault.

Hae-June, Hyo Jung,

Have you heard the gentle whispers of spring? Think of a warm spring day. In the shade, there may be snow as white as snow, and far off in the distance the fields are green, and the entire world appears to sing praise. The ones in a hurry are the wildflowers, which bloom even with the snow still on them. The melting snow flows down to the brooks, rippling as it goes.

On a rainy summer day, go to the skyway on the mountaintop. Gaze from the octagonal pavilion to Samgaksan, also known as Bukhan Mountain. As the thick fog before you dissipates, the gray skyline gives way to towering a mountain peak. As the fog flows forth like water rushing forth from the river, the mountainside displays its brawny body and the mountain peak peeks out, coquettishly. The mountainside and the mountain peak play hide-and-seek, when the fog covers its beauty again. At long last, the fog recedes and the mountaintop will appear before you again. The flowing fog will grab at the mountainside and start dancing. It will appear as though the entire mountain joins in on the dancing.

Aha! Could not this beautiful sight be compared to a painting on a summer's day?

Hyo Sung, Hae-Yeon,

What does autumn look like?

Run by a highway. The golden light shines on the golden field and sways before the leaves of the tarnished sunset and the green pine groves. The golden light of the fields stands in stark contrast to the reddish leaves and it appears to sing praise for the bountiful harvest that is to come.

The cars rush by, and I move too, and in the far-off distance, the fiery red leaves grow ever closer. The golden fields recede, and then only the evergreens remain. The strange contrast between the light and the shade is a gift from the gods, a gift from Heaven itself.

The snow falls. Large snowflakes fall without sound. On the golden fields, over the leaves bursting with reddish colors, even the imposing mountain peak is covered by snow. The whole world seems to be awash with snow, and all of Creation seems to bow to it. With it, silence, and a dignity that overcomes everything. There is no sound when snow falls. It can fall as high as a mountain and yet remain silent. How perfect.

The wind blows. Every branch where the snow has fallen disappears into the mist. Large chunks of snow also fall. The heavy silence breaks. Is it the wind or the sound of the snow falling?

So it follows that the wind transports us to the past, and the world returns to its rightful place, in the ancient past. Water is not sound, nor is snow. A heavy silence follows. I, as Grandfather Park, can hear the rich and full sound of the angels' singing, right at the beginning of the world's creation.

Praise the Earth. It is home to a place where so many billions have lived and died and will live. It is Mother to us all. Praise the sun. It is the Father of all creation.

To relate another anecdote from my life, I'd like to talk about the time I was in Frankfurt, Germany, for the construction of a steel mill.

At the time, I was traveling with two companions, both skilled employees of mine. Germany has a reputation for having lots of fairs, and during the peak season, it's difficult to make hotel reservations. In cases like these, we would board at a hotel about an hour or two away by train; in a small town. I believe this must have been the case.

The two began to exhibit symptoms of boredom and seemed cross. For them, business trips abroad had always been about international flights followed by company cars, and not trains. Small wonder why they were tired and a bit bored, for they had just spent over ten hours getting to Frankfurt and had to go by train for another one to two hours to reach the hotel.

I, instead, spent my time initially gazing out the windows, and taking in the sight of Germany's small villages. For me, I was accustomed to city vistas (en route to the hotel accommodations) after a flight, and this was a welcome change. A bare tree caught my attention, so it must have been in the depths of winter. For the two employees I brought with me, as soon as I saw them squirming in their respective seats, I began to speak to them, out of annoyance.

I pointed to the trees, so prevalent in that part of Germany, and said, "Look closely at those trees over there. They're different from the trees in Korea. Look how the tree trunks and the branches have beautiful symmetry."

"Now look at the lone tree over there. It is just the right width and circumference and observed from all sides and up, it is of the right length. Look at the branches, which are also just the right size and length. Look again at their symmetry. Is this not absolute beauty? Look out the window, at the trees and the towns and the far-off horizon…is this not a beautifully poetic scene?"

We disembarked a few moments later…but after this lecture, both of the employees would bring this up any time business trips were discussed…they would recall it and remember it with gratitude.

An enjoyment of life can be found in all sorts of things.

In your home, it's best to install an excellent audio system. And if you are able, I suggest the more expensive ones. These days, with cassette tapes and CDs, etc. the quality of the music is incomparable to what we used to have in the past; the quality of the music is outstanding. Some might say these new sound systems can rival a concert hall. The radio is fine (FM broadcasts) but there are too many skits for my liking.

When you are listening to music, do not be a silent audience member, but become a musician yourself. In my head, I imagine myself as a member of the symphony orchestra. I can become the cellist or the trumpet player. What about imagining yourself as the first chair violinist?

I myself like to imagine being the drummer. I become like one with the orchestra and move my hands to the beat. The melody flows and fills my heart, and I am involved in every note. In the melody, which rises and falls with the notes, I feel like my soul reverberating.

I am a believer that music is God's voice, speaking through instruments made and played by human hands.

My dear Hyo Jung, the second eldest of my granddaughters, used to listen only to Vivaldi's *Four Seasons* until she was two years old. Her mother used to say that Hyo Jung would stop crying once her mother turned this on.

Is the enjoyment of life limited to music? No, for it can be found in dance as well.

This is from a long time ago, but think of the 1988 Seoul Olympics. The Soviet Union gave us a cultural spectacle that left Koreans speechless. The music, the dancers, and the choir were brilliant. Of course, they are also known for the Bolshoi Ballet, which overwhelms the viewers. This was when our ballet companies were lagging far behind. The viewers all cried at one particular solo by Nelly Lee, a Korean-Russian. The rich cultural heritage of Russia shocked us all and left us deeply moved.

But the shock I received was not cultural but political. It's problematic that the viewers were left in tears, but I feared a conspiracy by the organizers. Now, the Soviet Union no longer exists, but communism is alive and well in China and North Korea.

Communism is scary. No matter how much the world changes, I cannot espouse a political system that stresses a materialistic view of society, and world domination.

To me, it's like a lion or tiger trying to turn into a lamb or doe. For the latter, they are not herbivores, but the communists, I fear, are lions and tigers, who eat other animals.

Singing and dancing, cultural spectacles, and all a part of showcasing communism. Sports is another arena where they can do this. I have spent over twenty years as an IAAF (now World Athletics) council member, and know some of what goes on behind the scenes. For communists, remember that they have the ultimate goal of propagandizing their political system through various means like what I detailed above, so please be careful.

Hitler was a Wagner• enthusiast. But he is responsible for the deaths of so many. For dictators, even music becomes a political tactic.

The pursuit of beauty is a joyful action that breathes life into our lives. One blade of grass, one grove of trees, the stoic stones nearby... when you gaze at these things, are they not beautiful? You can find the beauty in the most ordinary of things. There are many beautiful things in this world.

However, in the midst of all this beauty, you must also exist. You have to exist next to the stoic boulders and gaze at the beauty of Mount Seorak. If you do not exist, then the beauty of Mount Seorak does not diminish or increase, but the subject is yourself; beauty is secondary. It's not that the boulder is beautiful because it is over there, it is beautiful because I feel it to be so. When you gaze at the beautiful tree, then paint it on canvas, it becomes a different type of beauty.

Feeling joy by looking at something beautiful pales in comparison to the beauty that you create. If looking at and hearing beautiful things brings you joy, then the creation of something beautiful will give you even more pleasure.

• Wilhelm R. Wagner (1813–1883), was a German composer. Other than opera, he left large operettas in his wake, most of them written by him alone. They incorporated a lot of music and artistic theory. His famous works include *Bridal Chorus, Parsifal, Tristan and Isolde*, among others.

And Where Has This Great Man Come From?

"Work" is another blessing for Man. You plan and argue while working. When the work is completed, the sense of accomplishment you feel is one of the many gifts bestowed on the living. I live to work, and live to help others, and is this not one of the mantras I live by that I mentioned in previous chapters?

For people, they have to experience the right amount of discomfort. The discomfort will give them a drive to do something about it. Without the drive and the desire to do something, a person may as well be a corpse.

"If you do not wish to live for the next five years, run every day."

I say this back and forth with my friends.

When a healthy, normal person retires, you may see him some months later reduced to an old man, and given time, you may hear the news of his death.

A person must have work, as a stimulus. When you leave the workplace, then you should even create a new job for yourself. If you do not have a taut current of energy running through you, then you will wilt and bid farewell to the living sooner rather than later.

The following is a story told by Hyunju's father, one of my favorite friends:

"In western Canada, an aquarium sent fish from the Pacific Ocean all the way to the other side of the country. Upon arrival, when they checked on the fish, they were horrified to discover that all of them had died.

It wasn't the same country, but from the West Coast to the East Coast in Canada, the width of the country must be at least 3,000 miles long.

The aquarium's employees were perplexed. They came up with other ways to transport the fish but they were inadequate. After a while, someone came up with a rather brilliant idea: put some carnivorous fish in with the others, then send them to the other side of the country.

And guess what happened after that. Most of them were still alive after they were transported. This is the effect of feeling afraid. With predators threatening to eat them, they fought to live by running away. The other fish in the first transport had died because they were bored and felt suffocated, but with the inclusion of the mean fish, there was no time to feel boredom. They didn't want to die. This is what I mean by 'life.'"

Life always requires a stimulus, and the stimulus will bring about action, and work, and health. Am I not right, a hundred times over, that living to work like I do is a great formula for dealing with the minutiae of life?

In the midst of it all is your conscience.

Even if I don't mention it, you all should have a ready-made conscience. This is what God has buried in your hearts, from early on. Your conscience is always whispering to you, furtively. You should be able to distinguish between what is right or wrong.

Good works make people happier. This is because of one's conscience. If you do bad things, you get depressed. This is also because of one's conscience.

If you want a clean, pure, and joyful heart, you should always listen to your conscience. If you follow your conscience's lead, then you will find the joy required to live happily.

While you work, you will find that sometimes it will go well, and other times, not so well. You should not expect to succeed all the time.

Almost anyone works their hardest to succeed. But not all goes according to plan. As good and evil coexist, success and failure are close friends. That is why failure is said to be the boss of lessons learned. Do not fear failure. Failure is a good teacher and it will teach you how to succeed later.

In 1973, Grandpa had to retire from the South Korean Army.

Until this point, I had been very successful, and it was the first time in my life I had experienced despair. I cried a lot. And I learned a lot.

But then, as is now, Grandma never spoke about my failure, nor did she blame me for it. In a family, for my generation, at least, in a home, a husband and a father live off of power and self-esteem. You must take heed to not hurt their feelings, for they wound easily.

If you can, empathize with the despair of the man who failed. He will be experiencing self-loathing, which he is attempting to suppress. Others' criticisms and blame will probably fall on deaf ears.

Do not poke fun at the failures of other people.

Hae-June and Hyo Jung, when in the future you start families, remember this warning.

You should never speak of your husband's failure(s). You should always respect him and give him hope, which will make him brave enough to overcome his failure(s). I was able to overcome failure and achieve great things later. This is all thanks to Grandma's respect for me.

The University of Chicago stands shoulder-to-shoulder with the Ivy League universities. The one who is credited with making this university so great was the former university president, Robert M. Hutchins, who rose to this position at the mere age of twenty-eight.

It's remarkable enough that Hutchins rose to this high position at such an early age, but he was brilliant in spearheading the work that needed to be done, was bold in his decisions, and pushed for some radical changes, which upset many people.

He even got rid of Soldier's Field which used to be a football field and established the world's first nuclear reactor at the site. He did it for the good of the university. So many people were fans of football and hated him for it, but he did it anyway. Most people still did not understand his audacity.

One day, one of the people who opposed the nuclear reactor (a rather famous person, back in the day), went to Hutchins' father.

He said to him, "You must stop your son. It's good to reform some things, but one must have some discernment."

"Really? Well, nobody kicks around a dead dog," he replied while ushering him toward the door.

Hutchins' father was actually proud of his son. Like father, like son.

If you are a pioneer of a new line of work, you may have some dissenters. The chorus of mean comments will grow the better you work.

Do not back down. If you heed everyone's admonishments, then remember the adage, "The ship is now headed towards the mountains."

Even I, when I was in the prime of my life, received complaints from people around me and even endured slander. But I stubbornly kept to my style of working. A long time has passed since then, and all those mean comments have now turned into praise. It's not because I excelled, but because I did the right thing.

When I submitted my resignation to KEPCO, I went to a Buddhist temple in South Jeolla Province, called the Songgwang Temple (Spreading Pine Temple). Luckily for me, a Buddhist monk whom I admired greatly, Hwae-Gwang, was already residing there.[•]

When he saw me, he said, "And where has this great man come from?"

A religious dignitary like him has a formidable mind, so a person like me felt flummoxed. I stared at him wordlessly and confusedly. Then I decided to bow to him, in the way our Korean ancestors used to.

"I followed the clouds," I said.

I said this somewhat unexpectedly.

At the said temple, the green tea is especially good. The monk set about making some green tea. As I drank with him, I confided to him what had happened since I had seen him last. After all that one-sided conversation, he finally said to me, "What bad luck, for talking whilst working. You should have worked silently. That is wisdom."

To this day, I don't know how to work without making some noise. There must be a way, as the wise monk once said. My failures speak for themselves.

The Sound of Water

At the Songgwang Temple, there is a brook you have to cross before entering through the gates. There is a small but beautiful stone bridge that allows one passage, that bubbles merrily below. In its waters, still live fish that during the twelfth century, chased away some thieves.

According to a monk named Hyunho,[••] the thieves force-fed the

• At the time, the head Buddhist monk at the temple was Hwae-Gwang (real name: Kim In-gyung). Born in 1924, he was from Gaechon that is now a part of North Korea. In 1947, he became a monk and died in 1996.

•• The monk Hyunho resided in Spreading Pine Temple (real name: Yun Jeong-su). Born in 1942, he was born in Naju, South Jeolla Province. In 1960, he received his religious orders in order to become a monk.

monk the cooked fish in order to humiliate him. Afterward, the monk went to the brook and did his business there.

But as soon as he started regurgitating the cooked fish, which came back to life and flopped around, the thieves, now frightened, prostrated themselves on the ground.

The fish that live there still, playfully swimming about in the water, are descended from these fish, called "joongtaegi."

The monk named Hyunho looked sincere.

One summer, when the famous Buddhist monk named Beopjeong• asked me, whilst crossing the bridge, "Is not the sound of the bubbling brook beautiful?"

I countered what he said by asking, "Is the sound of water flowing really sound?"

As soon as I had said this, the monk stopped walking and stared at me with a furrowed brow.

He ushered me into the room meant for guests. Then he asked me again, "What do you mean, that the sound of water is not sound?"

This Buddhist monk had written a book *The Sound of Water, the Sound of the Wind*, and lived by the philosophy of owning nothing. He was quite famous for this stance, actually.

The atmosphere seemed thick, although I had said this without much thought. How had we started traversing down this odd path, I wondered.

"If the sound of water isn't sound..." Monk Beopjeong said to me

• Beopjeong (1935–2010), born Park Jae-chul, was born in Haenam, South Jeolla Province. In 1953, he became a Buddhist monk. He also served as the editor-in-chief of *Bulgyo Shimun*, and the head of the Spreading Pine Temple. In 1997, he established the Gilsangsa Temple. His works include *Talk and Silence*, *The Sound of Water and the Sound of the Wind*, and *Owning Nothing*, among others.

with a solemn face.

I could not evade an answer. I gathered my thoughts. Then I started my argument, as though I was an empirical scientist.

"The sound of water is not really sound. I used to oversee work in construction and learned that from the perspective of architecture, what I said is true. A fountain, for example, is common in the Middle East, to cool the hot air, and for ornamental purposes in a garden, they usually place fountains in the center."

I continued.

"From a physical standpoint, it cannot be completely silent. That is why paradoxically, the sound the fountain makes ironically breaks the complete silence. It's like how we need white and black together, in order to explain the other. When young people go camping near a stream, some of them say that the sound of the brook prevents them from sleeping soundly."

The serious monk's face became even more serious. He invited me into his own quarters. The tea he made for us was delicious.

That day, the monk invited me to stay overnight.

But I said, "I will follow the clouds, and I will go now. I will bid you farewell now." I kowtowed and stepped out the door.

The next day, I heard that he wished to speak to me again, so I passed the gate and went to his residence again.

He had meant to give me a framed calligraphy piece, written in Chinese characters. This type of work can be called "hwadu," which emphasizes a certain topic. "Hwadu" is used during meditation by Buddhist monks to reach some kind of enlightenment.

"Shim Ma Mul," or "What is this?" is the easiest explanation for what the characters meant.

When I looked closely, he had used the wrong character for water.

There was an extra brushstroke near the top that shouldn't have been there.

The monk next to him, Hyunho, said as much.

Monk Beopjeong looked at him in bemusement and said, "It's wrong? Too bad, I can't do anything about it now," and laughed quietly.

Then he looked at me and said, "I wrote this last year, and for the past year, it has been at another place. I went to get it back some days ago." He pointed to the frame.

I was aghast. He had meant to give this to me, which meant that he knew in advance that I would visit him, all the way from Seoul.

"Take this 'Shim Ma Mul,' and use it as the topic of your meditation. One thought will lead to others, and so forth. It may help you reach true enlightenment."

I am a lazy student, and to this day, I have yet to start this Zen meditation.

If I am to work without making noise, I still have a long way to go.

Can You Make This Horse Fly?

Once upon a time, a man fought with the King and was sentenced to death. The man implored the King to spare him, and said to him, "If you give me one year of freedom, then I will teach your favorite horse to fly."

The king was surprised and intrigued, so he asked, "If a year passes and my favorite horse doesn't fly?"

The man said, "Then I will die willingly."

The King accepted his entreaty.

"If a horse manages to fly, then I can wait a year," the King said to himself. He laughed at the man in his head.

The other prisoners said to the man later, "What do you mean, that a horse will fly?" The man's reply staggered them all.

"In a year, who knows? The King might die. Or I might expire. Or the horse may die. In a year, who knows what might happen? Or what if by the next year, what if I really do make the horse fly?"

This is a story from the *Talmud*.

In all things, do not despair. How frightening is the line, "...what if by the next year, what if I really do make the horse fly?" This is self-aggrandization at work, foolhardy but brave. In life, sometimes this foolhardy self-confidence will save you.

In Greek and Roman mythology, does not hope to stay with Pandora, who opened the box?

Even in war, they stress will rather than military might. If you still have the will to fight, then even if you are currently on the losing end, the fight is not over. In warfare, there are incidents that serve as examples of this.

If you are the boss, then you must never lose your bravery. Ever. Do not give up. Do not despair. Do not give up, no matter what the circumstances. Always stay hopeful, and charge ahead.

When you think that you are going to die, this is the hurdle you must overcome. If you manage to overcome this hurdle and gather your remaining strength, then do not give in to the opposing side. Endure. You too, should remember that, "I too may be able to make a horse fly," and find bravery here. If you endure, you win.

You hear talk of those who have "woon," or good luck. And they also talk of those who do not have "woon." But do you think "woon" exists in a vacuum?

If you give up, "woon" will not be your friend. If you give up before "woon" has a chance to work, then it's all over. So how to make "woon" your friend? Pray. If you pray hard, then "woon" will follow. You must always believe and have hope, and pray, and wait.

Two rabbits are staring at each other across a brook. One is in a shady area, while the other one is in a sunny spot. To the rabbit in the sunny spot, all he can see is the fallen snow on the other side, but to the rabbit in the shade, all he can see is the sunny hill on the other side.

The one in the shade does not give up hope. He's hungry and starving so he emerges from the shade and starts eating the new shoots that have broken through the ground. This is because he looked at hope.

The rabbit in the sunshine is wondering when the snow will melt. He waits and waits. The snow on the other side does not seem to be melting, and he feels like he has to wait forever. He sees no hope. The rabbit in the sunshine expires in his burrow. For he had only looked at failure.

There are many natural laws governing the universe. It's not really for me to say, but one of these laws is that everything changes. The sky changes, the land changes, people change, and hearts change. In my opinion, everything is impermanent.

What people fail to realize is how to go with the natural flow of the universe. I bet we'll never reach this realization.

But as "what goes up, must come down." Please take this literally.

Do not give up. There is nowhere else for "woon" to go.

Do not despair. For "woon" is waiting by the door.

Once in a Lifetime

In traditional Japanese tea ceremonies, there is a term called, "ilgiilhwae." It means, roughly translated, "Once in a lifetime."

For example, if I am meeting with someone, then this meeting is precious for the other one is my guest, and this moment will never come again. For the owner as well as the guest, one should always behave impeccably. This is their teaching. But how is this only expressed perfectly in the "Dado (a ceremonial way of preparing and drinking green tea)?"

In this world, a man is born, lives for a long time, and dies. He comes, and leaves.

My father also came and went, and my mother also came and went. I am also consigned to the same fate. A person's life as well as time, flow by, and how is it that we came together as one family?

It is fated. When I think of this, my heart starts pounding.

My beloved angels, where have you come from?

Life is bound by moral laws, and this is where we start our fated journey. Your mother is precious and your father is also precious. There is a reason for this, that filial piety must be your very foundation.

Life is joyful and precious because of this type of love.

If we are to live once in this life, then how could we not but spend each moment with integrity and thankfulness in our hearts?

"Ilgiilhwae." Let us remember this in our heart of hearts. In all things, we must treat everything with this type of attitude. Especially in loving your parents without any reservations.

A person's true nature is revealed in how they treat their parents. A happy life is not far off.

Love the Lord Almighty.

There will be times in this life when you cannot find solace in anything.

"Come to me, all you who are weary and burdened, and I will give you rest" (Matthew 11:28).

March 2018
Jung-ki "Rocky" Park